IF THERE ARE NO MORE HEROES, THERE ARE HEROINES

A Feminist Critique of Corneille's Heroines: 1637-1643

Josephine A. Schmidt

Assistant Professor of French
California State College, Bakersfield

UNIVERSITY
PRESS OF
AMERICA

LANHAM • NEW YORK • LONDON

Copyright © 1987 by

University Press of America,® Inc.

4720 Boston Way
Lanham, MD 20706

3 Henrietta Street
London WC2E 8LU England

British Cataloging in Publication Information Available

Library of Congress Cataloging-in-Publication Data

Schmidt, Josephine Anne.
    If there are no more heroes, there are heroines.

    Bibliography: p.
    1. Corneille, Pierre, 1606-1684—Characters—Heroines.
2. Corneille, Pierre, 1606-1684—Characters—Women.
3. Heroines in literature. 4. Women in literature.
5. Tragic, The, in literature. 6. Feminism and
literature. I. Title.
PQ1782.S36   1987   842'.4   87-2169
ISBN 0-8191-6278-7 (alk. paper)

All University Press of America books are produced on acid-free
paper which exceeds the minimum standards set by the National
Historical Publication and Records Commission.

TO MY PARENTS

AND

MARIA TASTEVIN MILLER

"Le débris de l'empire a de belles ruines:
S'il n'a plus de héros, il a des héroines."

Attila, Acte I, Scène ii, 253-54

ACKNOWLEDGMENTS

I wish to acknowledge with deep appreciation the valuable information and suggestions made by former Professor Maria Tastevin Miller (1888-) without whose pioneering book, Les Héroines de Corneille (Paris: Edouard Champion, 1924), my own feminist research on Corneille's heroines would have been much more difficult. Her enthusiasm for my work and her friendship have served as a constant source of support.

To this day, she is living in Paris and is excited about this book. An MLA paper I delivered in 1984 in Washington, D.C., which explains how I discovered she was still living, is included in the Appendix of this book. It is my hope that her work will enter the mainstream of all future feminist critiques of Pierre Corneille's heroines.

Since the bulk of this work was originally done as a doctoral dissertation at the University of Virginia, I owe a deep debt to Professors Hugh M. Davidson, my dissertation director, David L. Rubin, Mary B. McKinley and Beth Bjorklund, my dissertation readers, for their valuable suggestions, insightful comments, and steady encouragement.

I would also like to thank Professor Harriet R. Allentuch, who I met briefly at the Fourth Berkshire Conference on the History of Women, for her encouragement as I was about to embark on this research. And, I owe a debt to Elaine Rubin, who, in her generosity, gave me a copy of her dissertation bibliography on female heroic imagery in seventeenth-century France.

A past debt is also owed to Susan E. McCue, a women's historian, who discussed feminist criticism with me throughout every stage of my work.

A present debt is owed to Reide L. Garnett for her encouragement and kind words urging me to publish this manuscript; to California State College, Bakersfield's Affirmative Action Faculty Development Grant, which helped me revise and update my research; and to Jacki Lawson, my typist, for making this manuscript a reality.

TABLE OF CONTENTS

INTRODUCTION

A frequent opening remark among scholars to justify the appearance of a new book on Corneille, is something like the following: "Seventeenth-century scholars may readily ask whether another book on Corneille is either necessary or desirable. Every year at least one book and countless articles are added to the already overwhelming Cornelian bibliography."[1] While it is true that the Cornelian bibliography is overwhelming, it is not insofar as Cornelian heroines are concerned.

In all of Corneille scholarship, there are only four books devoted exclusively to the author's female protagonists. The first is the 1898 dissertation of Charles Ayer entitled, The Tragic Heroines of Pierre Corneille. Ayer's study of Corneille's twenty-four tragic heroines has been judged "uneven" because of its descriptive rather than explanatory nature, and its "often unjustly harsh" criticisms of the heroines.[2] Although Ayer considers the heroines "automatic" figures ("The tragic heroines of Corneille were created according to a system. This system was their doom."),[3] he does demonstrate that they share many characteristics: their aristocratic birth, polite breeding, "gloire," pathetic side, and that there are even an "appropriate" number of heroines in each play. His attempt to understand Corneille's characterization of his heroines is ambitious, although the end result is too formulaic and superficial. Yet, Ayer's book provides us with a useful overview of the heroines, and an excellent point of departure for any study of them. Since Ayer's is the first detailed book on the heroines, it is unfortunate that his work has had little or no effect on Cornelian scholarship.

The second book, Jeanne Le Guiner's 1920 book, Les Femmes dans Les Tragédies de Corneille,[4] addresses the bias in male scholarship, primarily from the eighteenth to the beginning of the twentieth century, which claimed that all of Corneille's heroines were the same. To counteract this bias, Le Guiner urges critics to study each heroine individually, as she has done, and to avoid facile classifications or regroupements of the heroines.

Other strengths of her book are that she uses the term "femme forte" for a phenomenon that existed in the moral literature of the seventeenth century; she

1

identifies the reality of "idées préconçues" that existed in male scholarship predating her book; she depicts Corneille as fair in his characterization of women; she attempts to distinguish one heroine from the other; and finally, she praises the heroines for their lucidity.

Le Guiner's analyses are perceptive and sensitive when she pinpoints the tension in Chimène's role and demonstrates that it is due to the interior and exterior obstacles that she faces. She also states that Corneille chooses to keep love in his tragedies, that the strength of Sabine's role lies in the fact that it was pure invention on Corneille's part, and that Pauline is the heroine most deserving of our admiration.

The weaknesses in her book lie in its uneven and sometimes contradictory statements: she is attempting to counteract the treatment given to Cornelian heroines in past scholarship, and yet, she is harsh in her judgements of Sabine and sees her only as a passive heroine. Le Guiner also acquits Horace of his violent crime against his sister, Camille, because of her antipatriotic statements. As a critic, she can find no saving grace in Camille, who she considers a violent and impulsive character.

In the final analysis, Le Guiner seems to be at crosspurposes with her original aim to restore the heroines to a more authentic séparateness based on their individuality and uniqueness from each other.

The third book on the heroines is Maria Tastevin's Les Héroïnes de Corneille, published in 1924. Tastevin presents a penetrating psychological and moral analysis of six Cornelian heroines: Chimène, Camille, Emilie, Pauline, Cléopâtre, and Bérénice. By concentrating on six outstanding tragic heroines, she manages to describe their characteristics and explore their motivations and psychology from a female point of view. A sense of urgency pervades Tastevin's work when she attempts to negate a trend in Cornelian criticism, predating 1924, which reflects a harsh bias toward his heroines:

> Les héroïnes cornéliennes ont particulièrement à souffrir d'idées préconçues. De temps à autre, une voix s'élève en leur faveur, mais l'opinion courante n'en semble guère modifiée.

> Il est d'usage de répéter qu'elles sont
> trop viriles, trop grandiloquentes,
> trop orgueilleuses, en un mot, que ce
> ne sont pas de vraies femmes. . . . Je
> ne surprendrai sans doute pas mon
> lecteur en lui disant dès maintenant
> que mes conclusions ne conforment pas
> de tous points à l'opinion
> traditionnelle sur les femmes de
> Corneille.[5]

Tastevin mentions two points that are crucial for the present study of Corneille's heroines. The first is that of preconceived ideas ("idées préconçues") or bias, as mentioned by Le Guiner, and the second is traditional opinions of women ("l'opinion traditionnelle sur les femmes"), or stereotypes. Since Tastevin's critical inquiry primarily addresses Voltaire, Sarcey, and Lanson, it can safely be inferred that the bias and stereotypes of which she speaks are male. As a result, Tastevin is in the position of defending Cornelian heroines against male bias and male stereotypes of women.

The fourth and final book on Corneille's heroines is Mary Jo Muratore's, The Evolution of the Cornelian Heroine. Muratore's book is solid because it treats all of Corneille's heroines throughout his thirty-two plays. She is aware of the stereotypes that exist in scholarship when characterizing his heroines, such as, ". . . the heroine as simply the female counterpart of the Cornelian hero."[6] Muratore also faults any study of Corneille's heroines, which limits itself to plays written only between 1636 and 1643; however, the present study will demonstrate that there is value in this when treating the heroines from a feminist critical posture.

The strengths of her book are numerous. Muratore considers the heroines to be in constant evolution, which is a view in harmony with the present study. She emphasizes what Corneille considered heroic comportment in women at various stages of his career, rather than dwell on the establishment of one predominant characteristic found in the various heroines.

Muratore wrote her book in order to address the "paucity of critical agreement"[7] on Corneille's heroines. She is one of the first critics to state that Corneille was truly interested in female

3

psychology and that women are at the core of his drama.

Finally, Muratore, in 1982, has devised formulas, in a similar vein to Charles Ayer's 1898 book, that all of Corneille's heroines can be fit into four groups: the idealists, the public servants, the individualists, and the reactive heroines. These categories are highly useful and may be used as handy devices particularly when examining the role and importance of love in Corneille's plays; however, given the feminist nature of my study, I drew more heavily from Maria Tastevin's book and did not fully integrate Muratore's research into my own.

Despite the contributions of Ayer, Le Guiner, Tastevin, and Muratore, the fate of Cornelian heroines in scholarship is still bleak. Only in the past fifteen years have scholarly articles been appearing which propose a reevaluation of the heroines.[8] Ayer's work remains disregarded, Le Guiner's book is neglected, Tastevin's fine book has been largely ignored, or briefly consulted in studies centered on the heroes,[9] and Muratore's book is still too recent to affect scholarship on Corneille's heroines. Insofar as these biases affect Corneille's heroines, we believe that they have hindered our ability to perceive the heroines as strong and positive "images of women" in his theater.[10]

A Feminist Critique

Tastevin's emphasis on the reinterpretation of Corneille's heroines is most, of all four books previously mentioned, in harmony with current modes of feminist literary criticism. Her analysis of the heroines entailed three stages. First, she identified bias and stereotyping towards Corneille's heroines in male scholarship; then, she negated it through a detailed psychological analysis of each heroine; and finally, she defended the heroines by showing that their values are different from or opposed to those of the heroes. The nature of the present inquiry on Corneille's heroines derives from the tradition begun by Tastevin.

What will be undertaken here is a feminist "re-vision" of several Cornelian tragic heroines.[11] The main consideration of my work is, "the analysis of the 'image of women' . . . as it appears in works by male authors."[12] In this case, Corneille is the only

4

author whose works will be examined for their "image of women." Implicit in this type of analysis is, first and foremost, the idea that women be considered as a "separate cultural group."[13] When, in Cornelian scholarship, his heroines are overshadowed by emphasis on the heroes, or overlooked in studies that associate heroism with masculinity (especially in the works of Doubrovsky and Dort),[14] they, as female protagonists and representatives of the female sex, are being denied their right to exist as a separate group in the literature that reflects their society. Gerda Lerner insists that women be restored to their own status: "Women are a category unto themselves: an adequate analysis of their position in society demands new conceptual tools."[15] Another women's historian, Carroll Smith-Rosenberg, emphasizes the pitfalls of the continued denial of the separate status of women in society:

> But my criticism of the New Social History goes beyond the fact that it has failed to study a major segment of the population. In doing so, contemporary social historians have also ignored one of the most basic forms of human interaction--that between the sexes. The dynamics of female-male relations are central to our understanding of the family, the church, the school, and indeed of all social institutions.[16]

The questions raised by Smith-Rosenberg are highly pertinent to Corneille's heroines. They, as half of Corneille's creation, have been virtually ignored in male scholarship, or relegated to a less important status then their male counterparts. It seems futile to continue to interpret and measure the worth of the heroines in the light of male heroic ethics that value masculinity, without attempting to discover or reveal heroic codes and ethics that pertain to females alone. Before a female ethic can be described, it is necessary to focus on the bias in male scholarship that has prevented a more accurate understanding of Corneille's heroines, and that has failed to consider female protagonists as a group unto themselves.

There is a long tradition of male bias against Cornelian heroines in literary criticism. The earliest examples of it may be found in Georges de Scudéry's Observations sur le Cid (1637), when he

5

refers to Chimène as "une prostituée," "un monstre,"
"une parricide," and as an "impudique."[17] This kind
of male perspective on Chimène is deprecatory in
nature; Chimène is thought to be shocking and immoral
because her behavior does not conform to accepted
codes of female behavior ("les bienséances"), in her
century. In other words, her characterization does
not correspond to seventeenth century female
stereotypes.[18] Since Chimène is shown to inhabit a
patriarchal world in Le Cid, Scudéry is in fact saying
that Chimène's role is not suitable for the stage
because it violates the proper behavior assigned to
females in his century. Catharine Stimpson makes an
interesting point on women in "respectable"
literature: "Women, female characters, particularly
in 'respectable' literature, represent the principles
of submissiveness to power, of passivity, or both. . .
."[19] Through his harsh reaction to Chimène, Scudéry
is, in effect, indicating that Corneille is creating
female characters who do not conform to seventeenth
century norms for female behavior. As a result,
Scudéry, reveals his personal bias against Chimène
because, for a female, she is not passive enough for
his taste.

In more recent scholarship, examples of male bias
toward Corneille's heroines still persist. Couton's
bias is in the form of a double standard. He uses the
heading, "La trilogie des monstres," as a neat way of
grouping three heroines: Cléopâtre, Théodore, and
Pulchérie.[20] He considers these Cornelian heroines
monsters because they desire power avidly, and will do
anything to get it. Yet, no such epithet is applied
to the heroes when they sought power and laid aside
all thoughts of the consequences of their acts.
Schlumberger, like Scudéry, reveals his personal bias
against the heoines, and prefers using stereotypical
terms rather than exploring female characterization.
He refers pejoratively to Camille as "une amoureuse,"
to Emilie as being "froide," and to Pauline in the
following manner:

> Elle insiste un peu trop, à notre goût,
> sur sa vertu, sur sa noblesse d'ame,
> sur les feux qu'elle a étouffés:
> toutes choses que la délicatesse d'une
> femme doit suggérer sans les dire.[21]

Schlumberger's male bias, which indicates his
attitudes towards women, is self-evident in his
remark, "à notre goût." He is not representing the

tastes of seventeenth century spectators, but rather his own subjective views on women. His tendency is to dismiss heroines who are actually highly complex, because they do not correspond to his concept of a woman.

Another manifestation of male bias of a different kind can be found in Doubrovsky.[22] He also clings to stereotypes of female behavior and promotes a double standard, in favor of the heroes, in his work. His views on the heroines as marked by an extreme form of polarisation and rigidity.[23] In what seems to be a caricature of male/female roles, Doubrovsky states that it is impossible for Cornelian heroines to escape their female condition: "Cependant, il est impossible au principe féminin d'incarner le principe de Maîtrise authentique."[24] In his estimation, the heroines, as females, are doomed to weakness that is shameful: "Loin d'être l'héroine 'virile' souvent décrite, Chimène pleurera donc à travers toute la pièce,--symbole de la faiblesse honteuse, chez Corneille; elle pleurera. . . ."[25] For Doubrovsky, male/female roles in Corneille are strictly polarized.[26] Doubrovsky frequently judges the heroines from the point of view of being less than and inferior to the heroes. He also praises Corneille for keeping the sexes in their respective places: ". . . Corneille ne confond jamais les hommes et les femmes" unlike a modern existential thinker such as Simone de Beauvoir.[27] Doubrovsky seems to delight in the idea of a Cornelian world where males and females are locked in rigid stereotypes. His brand of bias is critical of any deviation from the norm of male/female characterization in Corneille. While Doubrovsky will contribute to a more complete understanding of the complexity of the male heroic quest, he gives us nothing more than a one-dimensional view of the heroines. He, like other Corneille scholars, interprets the heroines' behavior in accordance with male heroic ethics and makes no attempt to delve into the complexity of female characterization in Corneille.[28]

As a result of this type of bias against the heroines found in male scholarship, it will be necessary to attempt to negate it by focusing on the heroines in an effort to complete the picture and counteract the trend. In this sense, feminist criticism must attempt to negate these biases:

7

> Feminists believe that women have
> been locked off in a condition of
> lesser reality by the dominant
> patriarchal attitudes and customs of
> our culture. We find these attitudes
> and customs reified in the institutions
> of literature and literary criticism.
> Feminist critics . . . are engaged in
> negating these reifications.
> Thus, . . . we may describe
> feminist criticism as a mode of
> negation seen within a fundamental
> dialectic.[29]

If, at first, we must engage in 'negative thinking" by
identifying and exposing male bias, it is because we
recognize that in a patriarchy the status of women,
and their reflections in literature, are inferior to
those of men. Our task can then be seen as being
twofold:

> Thus, as feminist critics, our
> sensitivities must be negative in that
> we are saying no to a whole series of
> oppressive ways, images and falsehoods
> that have been perpetrated against
> women both in literature and in
> literary criticism. But, on the other
> hand, we must be sensitive, too, to the
> new imaginative perceptions, to the new
> shapes that are beginning to take
> form--partly as a result of our
> negations.[30]

We realize that through the negation of male bias in
criticism, and through the recognition of the fact
that Corneille's heroines were created in a
patriarchal society, it will then be possible to
concentrate on a "re-vision" of his tragic heroines.

If, for a moment, we glance at definitions of men
and women and hero and heroine in seventeenth century
dictionaries, it will be possible to draw some
conclusions on their status in that century. First,
let us compare the definitions of "Homme" and "Femme"
in the 1694 edition of the Dictionnaire de l'Académie
Françoise:

> Homme.s.m. Animal raisonnable. En ce
> sens il comprend toute l'espece
> humaine, & se dit de tous les deux

          sexes. . . .
          <u>Femme</u>.s.f. La femelle de l'homme.[31]

Accordingly,   in   these   definitions   "Homme"   is
considered a generic term for both sexes, and "Femme"
conforms to the Old Testament concept that woman was
derived from man. Next, the definitions of "Herōs"
and   "Héroïne"   in   Antoine   Furetière's   1690,
<u>Dictionnaire</u> <u>Universel</u>, are worthy of a comparison
with those in the 1694 <u>Dictionnaire</u> <u>de</u> <u>l'Académie</u>
<u>françoise</u>. In Furetière:

          <u>Héros</u>,m. C'estoit chez les Anciens un
          grand & illustre personnage qui quoy
          que de nature mortelle, passoit dans la
          creance   des   peuples   pour   estre
          partipant de l'immortalité, & ils le
          mettoient au rang des Dieux après la
          mort. . . .
               Les Héros estoient ceux qui par
          leur eloquence manoient les peuples
          comme ils vouloient leur donnant de
          l'horreur pour le vice, en même temps
          que par leurs paroles & exemples ils
          les portoient à la vertu.
          <u>Héroïne</u>,f. Fille ou femme qui a des
          vertus de Héros, qui a fait quelque
          action héroïque.[32]

and in the <u>Dictionnaire</u> <u>de</u> <u>l'Académie</u> <u>françoise</u>;

          <u>Héros</u>.s.m.   (L'H s'aspire)   Selon
          l'antiquité payenne ce titre se donnoit
          à ceux qui par une grande valeur se
          distinguoient des autres hommes. "Les
          Héros de l'antiquité.'   Il se dit
          encore aujourd'huy des hommes qui font
          des actions de valeur extraordinaire.
          "Ce General est un vray Herōs."
               Il se dit aussi quelquefois pour
          un homme qui excelle en quelque vertu.
          "C'est un Héros en pieté."
          <u>Héroïne</u>.s.f. (L'H ne s'aspire point)
          Femme qui a les qualitez des Héros.
          "C'est une héroïne."[33]

It is apparent from these definitions that "Héroïne"
is not only derived etymologically from "Héros,' but
also in meaning since a heroine was someone who either
had the virtues or, more generally, the qualities of a
hero.   It is noteworthy that through implication,

                          9

"Héros" and "Héroïne" signify the same possibilities for an active form of heroic behavior. However, a heroine is considered a _female_ hero and not a heroine in her own right. We can also infer from these definitions, the lesser status of females in the seventeenth century. Cheri Register stresses the importance of the status of women for feminist criticism: "To understand a female author--or character--completely, the critic must take into account the social and legal status of women in her society. Feminist criticism is ultimately cultural criticism."[34]

Despite the fact that women in the seventeenth century were socially and legally inferior to men,[35] there was much discussion going on surrounding what was known as the "woman question." This discussion "centered on conflicting assessments of the negative or positive influence women exerted on the French social structure in a time of apparent flux."[36]

If we examine a selective list of the title of political, social, and religious tracts published during the first half of the seventeenth century, we will see that the image of the heroic woman, particularly in theater, was of much importance to this discussion of women's status. Here is a list of some of these titles on heroic women: _Les Eloges et les vies des reines et des princesses et des dames illustres_ (1630); _Le mérite des dames_ (1640); _La Galerie des dames illustres_ (1643); _La femme généreuse_ (1643); _La Femme héroïque_ (1643); _Le Triomphe des dames_ (1645); _La Galerie des femmes fortes_ (1647); and also one title of a work published at a later date but which has an interesting theme: _Les Femmes héroïques, comparées avec les héros_ (1669).[37] It is evident that all of these discussions generated publications that were contemporary with Corneille's creation of his heroic women and may have had a strong impact on his plays.[38]

Several other factors make Corneille a particularly interesting author to re-view in an "image of women" inquiry. Not only was Corneille influenced by the salons of his time, but he was a friend, through correspondence, with the Abbé de Pure, one of the seventeenth century's most enlightened thinkers on the "woman question."[39] It has also been demonstrated by Doubrovsky that Corneille's theater is a battlefield for male/female principles ("le principe mâle de la Maîtrise et le principe femelle du

10

Sentiment").[40] The dialectic occurring in Corneille's plays between male and female principles may be linked with the discussion of the status of women in his century, which was also centered on this basic dialectic. It is not surprising that Corneille created some of the strongest and most positive female protagonists during a century when literature on the "woman question" was abundant. Lougee stresses the importance of the seventeenth century's discussion of women's status:

> A valid argument could be made that the roots of modern feminist ideology lie in seventeenth-century writings, even that all basic components of modern feminism developed more fully by later generations were present in these seventeenth-century treatises.[41]

With this connection in mind, an attempt to focus on several Cornelian heroines in light of the renewed interest in the "woman question" in the seventeenth century seems particularly promising for a feminist critique. Before I specify the exact period in Corneille's theater that will be studied here, and the heroines in question, it is necessary to explain some facts that affected the composition and evolution of his audience.

The Evolution of Audience (1600-1647)

Corneille was an "homme de théatre" and an "homme de métier"[42] who was a virtuoso throughout the rich and diverse practice of his dramatic art. The most essential consideration for the successful practice of his art was the principle of "plaire," or the pleasure of his audience. The tastes and dictates of Corneille's audience ("le Public"), were foremost to him as a dramatist. This is amply proven in his Trois Discours: his retrospective work on over thirty years of writing for the French stage. Hugh M. Davidson emphasizes the importance of "audience support" particularly for theater in the seventeenth century:

> It is obvious that the dramatic literature of any period tends, by its nature, to be dependent on audience support. In the seventeenth century, however, this condition is reinforced by special economic and social factors, with the result that the audience has

11

both in theory and in fact a decisive
role in the creation of literature.[43]

While Corneille's audience reception and support is
crucial to the success of his art, Davidson cautions
us that we should not exaggerate the power of the
audience to determine the value of the author's work:

> In any such set of complicated
> factors in which one element is
> dominant, as the audience is here, we
> expect a natural tendency toward some
> sort of balance, toward some limitation
> of the dominant principle. Great poets
> are not going to leave all decisions
> having to do with the value of their
> works up to their audiences.[44]

We will now examine the influence of the presence of
women in Corneille's audience on his theater.

The question of the occurrence and of the
suitability of theater attendance for women may be
answered by surveying the opinions of critics of
Corneille, and of theater historians. When writing
about the performances of plays during the first half
of the seventeenth century, and the probability of
finding women in the audience, Adam states that:

> Une honnête femme, avant 1630, n'allait
> pas au théâtre. Des dames pourtant s'y
> risquaient, que Bruscambille interpelle
> dans ses Prologues. Croyons qu'alors
> elles portaient un masque, et pouvaient
> ainsi rougir à leur aise des
> plaisanteries incongrues qu'il
> débitait.[45]

He stresses that women who did attend the theater
before 1630 usually wore a mask or disguised
themselves in some way. When Brunetière writes about
the same period, the 1630's, he also makes remarks on
the presence of women in the audience: "Les dames,
qui jusqu'alors n'avaient guère fréquenté le théâtre,
commençaient à s'y montrer."[46] Lanson is more
definitive in his observations because he equates the
presence of women in the audience with a rise in the
popularity of the theater:

> La société polie s'accoutuma à venir
> occuper les loges; à la porte du

théâtre, certains jours, on vit dans la presse des <u>cordons</u> <u>bleus</u>. Enfin les dames ne craignirent plus se montrer à la comédie [comédie = play]. Il n'y s'y débita plus rien qu'une honnête femme ne put entendre: c'est-à-dire selon les bienséances de 1630 qui ne sont pas, tant s'en faut, celles de 1900. La présence habituelle des dames consacra la vogue du genre dramatique.[47]

He is in fact saying that polite society, that is, salon women and their followers, and other respectable women, attended the theater regularly. This was brought about, in part, by the "bienséances" of the 1630's which made their attendance possible and vastly improved the moral tone of the theater.

It appears that much progress was made during the 1630's for the renewed prosperity of the French theater. John Lough, an historian of seventeenth century theater, is emphatic on this point:

> It is indisputable that the theatre became much more fashionable in Paris by about 1630: the actors prospered, as two French companies were now permanently established in the capital. It is also an undoubted fact that gradually the theatre was to become much less coarse and that, from the aesthetic point of view, immense progress was to be made in the 1630's.[48]

He also lays much stress on the presence of respectable women in the audience around this time, and on the shift in the composition of the audience:

> It is generally accepted that the audience of the first twenty years of the seventeenth century was an almost entirely plebeian one, lacking the refining influence of the aristocracy, learned men (les doctes), and especially respectable women. The crude tastes of such an audience are, it is held, reflected in the extremely low aesthetic and moral standards of French drama in the opening decades of

13

> the century. Then, it is argued in the
> period between about 1625 and 1635 a
> revolution occurred in the composition
> of the audience; from being
> overwhelmingly plebian it became
> preponderantly aristocratic.[49]

It is significant that Lough connects the presence of
women in the audience with the improvement of the
moral tone of the plays performed. What seems likely
taking the above information into account, is that
Cardinal Richelieu's plan to rehabilitate the French
theater included his desire to gain the support of the
aristocracy ("learned men . . . and especially
respectable women"), in the theater audiences.

The fact that women gain access to the theater
around the time that Corneille began composing his
tragedies in the late 1630's is an important aspect of
the improvement that took place in his theater.[50] The
development of polite society with its emphasis on
refined behavior and language ("les bienséances") and
the theme of love and its psychology helped transform
French theater and had a lasting effect on Corneille's
plays. It is also necessary to stress the influence
of the salons on Corneille's work once the presence of
respectable women in his audience was an habitual
occurrence.

At the same time that women were present in
sizable numbers in Corneille's audience, they were
also entering the acting profession. Both Lancaster
and Descotes stress that women, though few in number,
began to enter or become important to the
profession.[51] We must not forget that this profession
afforded actors a highly unstable lifestyle, few
monetary rewards, and a poor moral reputation.
However, we can assume that with the "audience
support" from women, came the increasing presence and
support for actresses on the stage.

In his work on "La Préciosité," Lathuillère
devotes an entire chapter to Corneille in an effort to
establish the relation between the influence of the
salons on Corneille's theater and of Corneille on the
"Précieuses": the women who frequented the salons.
Lathuillère states that:

> Plus que dans des relations
> personnelles, plus encore que dans de
> petits vers d'ailleurs tout à fait

14

caractéristiques, c'est dans son théâtre même qu'il faut chercher les raisons du succès de Corneille auprès des précieuses. De longue date, ses pièces ont plu aux dames.[52]

He informs us that two of the most important women authors of the seventeenth century, Madame de Sévigné and Madame de Lafayette were strongly influenced by Corneille's theater: "Mme de Sévigné incarne toute une génération pour laquelle le théâtre de Corneille, du Cid à Oedipe, représente cette aspiration vers la gloire, la grandeur, une sorte de pureté, inséparable de son idéal de vie."[53] Madame de Sévigné also wrote that she was "folle de Corneille" in one of her letters. And of Madame de Lafayette, Lathuillère insists that: "Elle reste toute sa vie une cornélienne convaincue."[54] He also confirms the extent of Corneille's influence on the "précieuses": "Ainsi, Corneille jouit d'une sorte de primauté dans les salons et particulièrement dans les salons précieux. Sa royauté est confirmée, pendant la décade qui suit, jusque vers 1670, par de nombreux écrits."[55] We must also not forget that in his poem "Excuse à Ariste," a précieux poem, Corneille claimed that his love for a woman was responsible for his first verses and his first play, Mélite.

Although love had been frequently neglected until Nadal, the love element is an important aspect of Corneille's theater:

> Si le règne de la préciosité a été celui de la femme, le théâtre de Corneille en offre déjà des exemples notables. Le héros d'ordinaire y fait preuve d'une soumission parfaite devant celle qu'il aime. Rodrigue a obéi au roi et, pour gagner Chimène, a affronté Don Sanche. . . . Pour laver son crime, il est pret à accomplir toutes ses volontés et même à mourir si elle le lui ordonne.[56]

It is present throughout Corneille's thirty-two plays; however, only his tetralogy: Le Cid, Horace, Cinna and Polyeucte concern us in this inquiry. It is of major relevance to this study of five Cornelian heroines, whose creation spans the period from 1637-1643, that all the factors pertaining to the presence of respectable women in Corneille's audience and their influence on his theater be kept in mind during the following textual analysis.

If we are to examine the "image of women" in four Cornelian plays, it seems most challenging to choose his four best known tragedies. Although these plays have generated much critical interpretation over the centuries, Corneille's female protagonists continue to be overshadowed by analyses of the heroes. It is my belief that if we restore the heroines to their dramatic context in the text, we can best negate the trend of male bias. It will then be possible to concentrate our energies on the perception of a female ethic, which governs the behavior of the heroines, and which the heroines are in the process of creating from one play to the next.

The five heroines who will be studied here are: Chimène in Le Cid; Camille and Sabine in Horace; Emilie in Cinna; and Pauline in Polyeucte. A three part outline will be proposed for the textual study of each heroine's role. The first part entitled: "The Creation of a Female Ethic," includes a look at the heroines' reaction to the dominant male ethic, their response to it, and the qualities that characterize them as strong images of women. The second part: "The Heroines' Effect on Tragic Theory," attempts to restore the connection between the presence of women in Corneille's audience and the effect of their themes on tragic theater. The third part: "The Fate of the Heroine," will examine the dénouements of all four plays for the outcome of each heroine's struggle against the male ethic. This final section will also entail a look at verbal references to the heroines which indicate their fate by the dénouement. This section will be of the utmost importance for our ability to draw conclusions on the authenticity of Corneille's five heroines as accurate "images of women."

Georges de Scudéry's and Jean Chapelain's Views on Chimène

Before any reexamination of the role of Chimène in Le Cid, it is necessary to reevaluate the attitudes towards Chimène in two central seventeenth century critical texts. These two texts began a trend in Cornelian criticism which greatly hindered accurate appraisals of Cornelian heroines, i.e., appraisals of the heroines in light of the fact that male and female

16

heroic values were distinct in the society and literature of the seventeenth century.[57]

The two critical texts that will be examined for their views on Chimène are, in order of composition: Georges de Scudéry's, Observations sur Le Cid (1637), and Jean Chapelain's, Les Sentimens de L'Académie Françoise sur la Tragi-Comedie Du Cid (1637).[58] The crucial difference between these texts is that the former represents a spiteful and embittered attack on Le Cid by an individual, whereas the latter attempts a critical appraisal of Le Cid, in the light of classical dramatic aesthetics, by Chapelain, a representative of the then newly founded Académie Française, which attempted to establish a seventeenth century poetics for the theater. Therefore, Chapelain's text is much more official in tone; however, both critics categorically uphold accusatory views on Chimène's "immorality" as a tragic heroine, and they both concur in their belief that Chimène consents to marry her father's murderer.

Georges de Scudéry's Observations sur Le Cid set the tone for generations of Cornelian scholars who, like Scudéry, blame Chimène for consenting to this marriage. Does Chimène really consent to it or is she tricked or coerced into agreeing to it? Have critics beginning with Scudéry examined the dénouement of Le Cid carefully enough? Also, why are Chimène's role and morals so closely scrutinized and severely judged by Scudéry and Chapelain? These questions will be kept in mind as we examine Scudéry's and Chapelain's views on Chimène.

In the Observations sur Le Cid, Scudéry's first reference to Chimène implicitly illustrates how the morality of the heroine must be aligned with the moral dictates of seventeenth century codes of female behavior:

> . . . il n'est point vray-semblable qu'une fille d'honneur, espouse le meurtrier de son Pere. . . . je ne croy pas qu'il suffise, de donner des repugnances à Chimene; de faire combatre le devoir contre l'amour; de luy mettre en la bouche mille antitheses sur ce sujet; ny de faire intervenir l'authorité d'un Roy; car enfin, tout cela n'empesche pas qu'elle ne se rende parricide, en se resolvant

17

d'épouser le meurtrier de son Père.
. . . enfin Chimene est une parricide.
. . .⁵⁹

As stated by Scudéry, Chimène's behavior is neither
suitable nor believable for "une fille d'honneur" when
she marries her father's murderer.[60] Chimène's role
makes her repugnant. Scudéry strongly stresses this
when he calls her "une parricide" by "se resolvant
d'épouser le meurtrier de son Père." The words that
are questionable are: "en se resolvant." Does
Chimène clearly make up her mind to marry Rodrigue?
Is it her choice? Is she really "une parricide"?
Scudéry is accusing Chimène, a character in a play, of
making decisions that are not hers to make. Chimène,
as will be evident in the textual interpretation of
her role, is not in a position to determine her own
fate, but dependent on her father's will or the
king's. Therefore, the accusation that Chimène firmly
made up her mind to marry Rodrigue is both absurd and
inaccurate in relation to the development of her
character in Le Cid.

For Scudéry, Chimène's character not only
violates female morality, the social codes of
behavior, and the doctrine of verisimilitude, but also
the social and literary "bienséances."[61] As stated by
Milorad Margitíc: ". . . la conduite de l'héroïne est
objet de certains tabous, codifié par la 'bienséance'
du 'sexe.' . . ."[62] Scudéry states that Chimène's
marriage to Rodrigue might have been historic and
true: "mais non pas vray-semblable, d'autant qu'il
choque la raison et les bonnes moeurs. . . ."[63]
Implicit in "les bonnes moeurs" is the fact that a
code which dictated socially acceptable behavior for
females existed for a woman of Chimène's social rank.
Scudéry also finds fault with Chimène for violating
that code. In a heavy-handed fashion, he blames
Chimène for her unnatural behavior:

> . . . l'on y voit une fille desnaturée
> ne parler que de ses follies,
> lorsqu'elle ne doit parler que de son
> malheur, pleindre la perte de son
> Amant, lors qu'elle ne doit songer qu'a
> celle de son pere; aimer encor ce
> qu'elle doit abhorrer; souffrir en
> mesme temps, et en mesme maison, ce
> meurtrier et ce pauvre corps; et pour
> achever son impieté, joindre sa main à

celle qui dégoute encor du sang de son
pere.[64]

The epithet "desnaturée" is one that has persistently
been used in Cornelian criticism when referring to
Chimène. Scudéry develops his argument against
Chimène: ". . . un Roy caresse cette impudique; son
vice y paroist rescompensé, la vertu semble bannie de
la conclusion de ce Poeme. . . ."[65] Not only is
Chimène "une parricide," a "desnaturée" and an
"impudique," but also a monster:

> Mais je descouvre encor des
> sentimens plus cruels et plus barbares,
> dans la quatriesme Scene du troisieme
> Acte, qui me font horreur. C'est où
> cette fille (mais plustost ce monstre)
> ayant devant ses yeux Rodrigue encor
> tout couvert d'un sang qui la devoit si
> fort toucher. . . .[66]

When commenting on Chimène's "immorality," Scudéry is
horrified by Chimène's violation of society's code of
suitable female behavior. Scudéry continually
emphasizes Chimène's sex and her bold speech which is
incongruous with her sex:

> . . . lors que Chimène dit que Rodrigue
> n'est pas Gentilhomme, s'il ne se vange
> de son pere; ce discours est plus
> extravagant que genereux, dans la
> bouche d'une fille, et jamais aucune ne
> le diroit, quand mesme elle en auroit
> la pensee. . . . Les plus critiques
> trouveroient peut-estre aussi que la
> bienseance voudroit, que Chimène
> pleurast enfermee chez elle, et non pas
> aux pieds du Roy, si tost apres cette
> mort. . . .[67]

Scudéry's accusations against Chimène have a snowball
effect. He compares her to a prostitute, after he has
already named her everything including "une Furie":

> . . . leur seconde conversation, est de
> mesme stile que la premiere, elle luy
> dit cent choses dignes d'une
> prostituée, pour l'obliger à batre ce
> pauvre sot de Don Sanche. . . .[68]

It seems that Scudéry has taken Chimène completely out
of dramatic context, as is the case with the Académie,
when he adds insult upon insult on her character. It
should not be overlooked, that, within the context of
the theater, Chimène was very well received by Anne of
Austria and the theater-going women of the seventeenth
century. Corneille himself reminds Scudéry of this
fact:

> Quand vous avez traité la pauvre
> Chimène d'impudique, de prostituée, de
> parricide, de monstre, ne vous
> êtes-vous pas souvenu que la Reine, les
> princesses et les plus vertueuses dames
> de la cour et de Paris l'ont reçue en
> fille d'honneur?[69]

Upon the request of Scudéry and with the approval
of Richelieu, Jean Chapelain undertook his criticism
of Le Cid,[70] and represented the Académie Française in
his Les Sentimens de l'Académie Françoise sur la
Tragi-Comedie Du Cid. Chapelain is even more
insistent than Scudéry on blaming Chimène for being
determined to marry her father's murderer: "Car ny la
bienseance des moeurs d'une Fille introduitte
vertueuse n'y est gardée par le Poëte, lors qu'elle se
resout à espouser celuy qui a tué son Pere. . . ."[71]
Once again the words that are highly questionable when
referring to Chimène's character are: "qu'elle se
resout." Does Chimène make up her mind freely to
marry Rodrigue or is this decision forced on her? It
is apparent from the text of the play that first Le
Comte has the power to determine his daughter's fate,
and that after his death Don Fernand, the king, has
authority over Chimène.

Chapelain, like Scudéry, lends much importance to
Chimène's role and its "immorality":

> . . . nous croyons qu'il y a eu encore
> plus de sujet de le reprendre pour
> avoir fait consentir Chimene à espouser
> Rodrigue le jour mesme qu'il avoit tué
> le Conte. Ce qui surpasse toute sorte
> de creance et qui vraysemblablement ne
> pouvoit tomber dans l'ame non seulement
> d'une sage Fille, mais de la plus
> despoüillée d'honneur et d'humanité.[72]

Chapelain agrees with Scudéry that Chimène sins
against the "bienséance" of her sex:

> L'Observateur [Scudery] apres cela
> passe à l'examen des moeurs attribuées
> à Chimene et les condanne. En quoy il
> nous a entierement de son costé, car au
> moins ne peut-on nier qu'elle ne soit
> Amante trop sensible et sans pudeur
> contre la bienseance de son sexe et
> Fille de mauvais naturel contre ce
> qu'elle devoit à la memoire de son
> Pere. . . . il est clair qu'elle ne se
> devoit point relascher dans la
> vengeance de la mort du Conte et bien
> moins se resoudre à espouser celuy qui
> l'avoit fait mourir.[73]

Once again Chapelain continues the use of "se
resoudre" when referring to Chimène's role in her
marriage. A tone of blame will continue in Les
Sentimens, when Chapelain in essence puts Chimène on
trial:

> Nous la blasmons seulement de ce que
> son amour prevaut sur son devoir et
> qu'en mesme temps qu'elle poursuit
> Rodrigue elle fait des voeux en sa
> faveur. Nous la blasmons de ce
> qu'ayant fait en son absence un bon
> dessein de le poursuivre de le perdre
> et de mourir apres luy si tost qu'il se
> presente à elle, quoy que teint du sang
> de son Pere, elle le souffre en son
> logis en dans sa chambre mesme. . . .[74]

Rodrigue's appearance in Chimène's house will be put
in perspective in the textual analysis of the play
since Rodrigue actually forced his way in without
Chimène's knowledge and without her consent. Chimène
is not only "cowardly" in her pursuit of Rodrigue, but
she also does not uphold the honor of her sex, which
should be much more severe in practice:

> Chimene au retour quoy que pour se bien
> ressentir de la mort de son Pere elle
> deust faire plus que Rodrigue pour
> venger l'affront du sien puis que
> l'honneur de son sexe exigeoit d'elle
> une severité plus grande et qu'il n'y
> avoit que la mort de Rodrigue qui peust
> expier celle du Conte, poursuit
> laschement cette mort, craint d'obtenir
> sa condamnation et se souvient trop

21

> qu'elle est Amante, c'est à dire n'a
> pas assez de soin de son honneur.[75]

Chapelain seems to imply that as a heroine, Chimène
should find an equivalent means to seek vengeance, and
that only Rodrigue's death should satisfy her. But
what of the paradox of Chimène's sex? When we examine
the text of the play, we will see that Chimène hardly
pursues Rodrigue's death "laschement." One of the
most distinctive attributes of Chimène is that despite
the limits imposed on her by the socio-political
context of seventeenth century society, she insists on
pursuing Rodrigue until she feels that her honor has
been defended. She in effect chooses action, not
tears and laments, to avenge her father's death.

Chapelain's condemnation of Chimène seems
illogical and absurd since Chimène does everything
feasible, for a female, to pursue her father's
murderer; and that it is obvious that within the
dramatic circumstances of the play, Chimène's position
is one of forced dependence and lack of tangible
power. When Chapelain blames Chimène for not publicly
opposing Don Fernand's ordinance:

> Quant à l'ordonnance de Fernand
> pour faire espouser Chimène à celuy de
> ses deux Amans qui sortiroit vainqueur
> du combat, elle ne scauroit passer que
> pour très-injuste et Chimène fait une
> très-grande faute de ne refuser pas
> ouvertement d'y obeir.[76]

It becomes apparent that Chapelain has lost sight of
the fact that Chimène is a character in a play.

It is very curious that both Chapelain and
Scudéry scrutinize and criticize Chimène's role most
severely, and condemn her and her creator for
immorality. It will be shown in this study of some of
Corneille's heroines that an important factor in
Corneille's originality is in the creation of his
heroines. Chapelain and Scudéry did, in fact,
inadvertently emphasize, through their negative
criticism, Corneille's originality with regard to
Chimène since the French stage had never quite
experienced before such a self-determining heroine.

As Couton pointed out, Corneille's adversaries
found something subversive in Le Cid:

Mais on n'a pas assez remarqué dans quelle situation délicate le mettaient ses adversaires. Leurs attaques le taxaient d'immoralité, pour un peu l'eussent accusé de saper la société familiale. En un temps de littérature dirigée et volontiers moralisante, ils le faisaient plus ou moins malignement apparaître comme un écrivain subversif.[77]

It is very significant for this study of Corneille's heroines that Chimène was judged "immoral" by Scudéry and Chapelain in that Chimène was considered subversive or, in other words, "unprecedented" for a heroine on the French stage of the 1630's. By concentrating on what is for them shocking in Chimène's role, Scudéry and Chapelain did in effect indicate where Corneille's originality lies. It will be shown that as a dramatist, Corneille's female characterization was actually highly original for his time, and his heroines found great favor among the theater-going women of the seventeenth century.

NOTES

1. See "Preface" Claude Abraham, Pierre Corneille (New York: Twayne, 1972).

2. David C. Cabeen, and Jules Brody, gen. eds. A Critical Bibliography of French Literature. Vol. III: The Seventeenth Century, ed. Nathan Edelman (Syracuse: Syracuse University Press, 1961), p. 204.

3. Charles C. Ayer, The Tragic Heroines of Pierre Corneille (Strassburg: Heitz, 1898), pp. 136; 141; 28.

4. Jeanne Le Guiner, Les Femmes Dans Les Tragédies de Corneille (Quimper: Imprimerie Vre Ed. Menez, 1920).

5. Maria Tastevin, Les Héroïnes de Corneille (Paris: Edouard Champion, 1924), pp. vi-vii.

6. Mary Jo Muratore, The Evolution of the Cornelian Heroine (Potomac, Maryland: Studia Humanitatis, 1982), p. 2.

7. Muratore, p. 4.

8. Harriet R. Allentuch, "Reflections on Women in the Theater of Corneille," Kentucky Romance Quarterly, Vol. XXI, No. 1 (1974), pp. 97-111; William Cloonan, "Women in Horace," Romance Notes, Vol. XVI, No. 3 (Spring, 1975), pp. 647-52; Wolfgang Leiner and Sheila Bayne, "Cinna ou L'Agenouillement D'Emilie Devant La Clémence D'Auguste," Onze Etudes sur l'Image de la femme, ed. Wolfgang Leiner (Paris: Jean Michel Place, 1978), pp. 195-219. Other articles that suggest that the heroines in Corneille be reevaluated that were not integrated into this book are: Bettina Knapp, "Pierre Corneille's Horace: Heroism? Sacrifice? - The Power Hungry," Classical and Modern Literature, Vol. 1, No. 2 (Winter, 1981), pp. 133-145; Mitchell Greenberg, "Horace, Classicism And Female Trouble," Romanic Review, Vol. LXXIV, No. 3 (May, 1983), pp. 271-292; Wendy Gibson, "Women And The Notion of Propriety In The French Theatre (1628-1643)," Forum For Modern Language Studies, Vol. XI, No. 1 (January 1975), pp. 1-14; Karolyn Waterson, "L'Utilité Dramatique De L'Infante De Corneille,"

Neophilologus, Vol. 64 (1980), pp. 182-185; Susan Tiefenbrun, "Blood And Water In Horace: A Feminist Reading," Papers on French Seventeenth Century Literature, ed. Wolfgang Leiner, Vol. X, No. 19 (1983), pp. 617-634; Serge Doubrovsky, "Corneille: masculin/féminin: réflexions sur la structure tragique," Papers on French Seventeenth Century Literature, ed. Wolfgang Leiner, Vol. XI, No. 21 (1984), pp. 89-121.

9. In their books on Corneille, André Stegmann, Serge Doubrovsky, Robert Nelson, and Mary Jo Muratore are the only Cornelian scholars who include Tastevin's book in their bibliographies.

10. Feminist critics recognize "that each person 'sees' phenomena through a filter of concerns and awarenesses. . . . For this reason we pose a challenge to the assumption that any scholar is free from ideological bias or value preference." Josephine Donovan, "Afterword: Critical Re-vision," in Feminist Literary Criticism, p. 76.

11. The splitting of the word revision to "re-vision" is a commonplace in feminist criticism. It stresses the need to employ a methodology with a new way of looking at literature with the "image of women" in mind.

12. Cheri Register, "American Feminist Literary Criticism: A Bibliographical Introduction," in Feminist Literary Criticism, ed. Josephine Donovan (Lexington: University Press of Kentucky, 1975), p. 2.

13. Josephine Donovan, "Afterword: Critical Re-Vision," in Feminist Literary Criticism, ed. Josephine Donovan (Lexington: University Press of Kentucky, 1975), pp. 77.

14. See Serge Doubrovsky, Corneille et la dialectique du héros (Paris: Gallimard, 1963), and Bernard Dort, Pierre Corneille: dramaturge (Paris: L'Arche, 1957).

15. Gerda Lerner in "The Feminists: A Second Look," Columbia Forum, 13 (Fall, 1970): 24-36, as quoted by Joan Kelly-Gadol in "The Social Relation of the Sexes: Methodological Implications of Women's History," Signs: A Journal of Women in

Culture and *Society* (Summer, 1976), Vol. 1, No. 4, p. 814.

16. Carroll Smith-Rosenberg, "The New Woman and the New History," *Feminist* *Studies*, Vol. 3, No. 1/2 (Fall, 1975), p. 189.

17. Georges de Scudéry, *Observations* *sur* *le* *Cid* (1637), pp. 71-111, in *Armand Gasté, La Querelle du Cid: Pièces et Pamphlets* (Genève: Slatkine Reprints, 1970).

18. On the "use of female stereotypes as tools in sex-role socialization" in literature, see Cheri Register, "American Feminist Literary Criticism: A Bibliographical Introduction," in *Feminist Literary Criticism*, pp. 6-7.

19. Catharine R. Stimpson, "Sex, Gender, and American Culture," in *Women* *and* *Men:* *Changing* *Roles,* *Relationships,* *and* *Perceptions*," eds. Libby A. Cater, Anne Firor Scott, et al. (New York: Praeger Publishers, 1977), p. 222.

20. Georges Couton, *Corneille* (Paris: Hatier, 1958), p. 111.

21. Jean Schlumberger, *Plaisir* *à* *Corneille* (Paris: Gallimard, 1936), p. 94.

22. Serge Doubrovsky, *Corneille* *et* *la* *dialectique* *du* *héros* (Paris: Gallimard, 1963).

23. Of women in English literature, Catharine Stimpson says, "Women, when they are present, tend to have polarized roles, which provoke polarized judgements. They represent extremes; they are, for example, either very good or very bad." See "Sex, Gender, and American Culture," in *Women* *and* *Men*, p. 221.

24. Serge Doubrovsky, *Corneille* *et* *la* *dialectique* *du* *héros*, p. 388.

25. Doubrovsky, p. 111. (The underlined word represents Doubrovsky's use of italics.)

26. Doubrovsky, see p. 121.

27. Doubrovsky, p. 133. Doubrovsky's criticism of Simone de Beauvoir seems unfair or misplaced

because he is probably referring to her book Le Deuxième Sexe (1949) and not her existential writings when he chastises her for not keeping the sexes in their "respective" places.

28. William O. Goode comes immediately to mind when he places Chimène in the "nonheroic, the common order" because he believes that she fails to "integrate" into the dominant male heroic ideology represented by Rodrigue. See "Hand, Heart, and Mind: The Complexity of the Heroic Quest in Le Cid," PMLA, Vol. 91, No. 1 (January, 1976), p. 45.

29. Josephine Donovan, "Afterword: Critical Re-vision," in Feminist Literary Criticism, p. 74.

30. Josephine Donovan, p. 76.

31. S. V. "Homme"; "Femme," in Le Dictionnaire de l'Académie françoise (Paris: Académie françoise, 1694).

32. S. V. "Héros"; "Héroine," in Dictionnaire universel by Antoine Furetière (Paris, 1690).

33. S. V. "Héros"; "Héroine" in Le Dictionnaire de l'Académie Françoise (Paris: Académie françoise, 1694).

34. Cheri Register, "American Feminist Literary Criticism. . . ." in Feminist Literary Criticism, p. 10.

35. On Salic law, which excluded women from the right of succession to the French throne, see Elaine R. Rubin's dissertation, "The Heroic Image: Women and Power in Early Seventeenth-Century France, 1610-1661" (Diss. George Washington University, 1977). Rubin also stresses the inferior legal status of women in that century. See also, for a discussion of the inequality in male/female education in the seventeenth century, Elfrieda T. Dubois, "The Education of Women in Seventeenth-Century France," French Studies, Vol. XXXII, No. I (January, 1978), pp. 1-19; Roger Duchêne, "L'Ecole des Femmes au XVIIe Siècle," Mélanges offerts à Georges Mongrédien (Limoges: Soc. d'Etudes du XVIIe Siècle, No. II, 1974), pp. 143-172.

36. Carolyn C. Lougee, Le Paradis des Femmes: Women, Salons and Social Stratification in Seventeenth Century France (Princeton: Princeton University Press, 1976), p. 5.

37. Maité Albistur et Daniel Armogathe, Histoire du Féminisme Français: du moyen age à nos jours (Paris: Editions des Femmes, 1977), 12-23; Ian MacLean, Woman Triumphant: Feminism in French Literature, 1610-1652 (Oxford: Oxford University Press, 1977), p. 231.

38. Elaine R. Rubin, Ian MacLean and Carolyn C. Lougee give ample evidence of the treatises, pamphlets, tracts, etc., published during Corneille's dramatic career. Of their probable effect on his work, see Rubin and MacLean.

39. See Roger Lathuillère, La Préciosité. Etude Historique et Linguistique. Vol. I (Gêneve: Droz, 1966), pp. 452-531.

40. Doubrovsky, p. 207.

41. Carolyn C. Lougee, Le Paradis des Femmes, p. 7.

42. Marie-Odile Sweetser, La Dramaturgie de Corneille (Genève: Droz, 1977), p. 17.

43. Hugh M. Davidson, Audience, Words, and Art. Studies in Seventeenth-Century French Rhetoric (Columbus: Ohio State University Press, 1965), p. 143.

44. Davidson, p. 143.

45. Antoine Adam, Histoire de la Littérature Française au XVIIe Siècle, Vol. I (Paris: Editions Mondiales, 1962), pp. 173-4. See also, W. L. Wiley, The Early Public Theatre in France (Cambridge: Harvard University Press, 1960), p. 207.

46. Fernand Brunetière, Etudes Critiques sur l'Histoire de la Littérature, Vol. 6 (Paris: Hachette, 1911), p. 139.

47. Gustave Lanson, Corneille (Paris: Hachette, 1898), p. 31. See also W. L. Wiley, p. 210.

48. John Lough, Paris Theatre Audiences in the Seventeenth and Eighteenth Centuries (London: Oxford University Press, 1957), p. 43.

49. Lough, p. 4.

50. Lough, pp. 13-14. The "greater refinement, both in manners and language . . . was spread among the upper classes of French society by the development of social life in the salons." This factor along with the "cult of the bienséances" improved the type of play that took place.

51. Henry C. Lancaster, A History of French Dramatic Literature in the Seventeenth Century. Part I: The Pre-Classical Period 1610-1634, Vol. II (Baltimore: The John Hopkins Press, 1929), pp. 726-52; Maurice Descotes, Les Grands Roles du Théatre de Corneille (Paris: Presses Universitaires de France, 1962), p. 23. See also Lancaster (p. 713), where he emphasizes that with the improvement in the tone of the stage came a large number of people of refinement who influenced the type of play performed and the quality of acting.

52. Roger Lathuillère, La Préciosité. Etude Historique et Linguistique, Vol. I (Genève: Droz, 1966), p. 463.

53. Lathuillère, p. 467.

54. Lathuillère, p. 467.

55. Lathuillère, p. 466.

56. Lathuillère, p. 471; Octave Nadal, Le sentiment de l'amour dans l'oeuvre de Pierre Corneille (Paris: Gallimard, 1948), pp. 33-165; 254-67. See also an important article on "Corneille et 'L'Astrée'" by E. Droz in Revue d'Histoire Littéraire 28 (1921), pp. 161-203; 361-87.

57. See Ian MacLean, Woman Triumphant: Feminism in French Literature 1610-1652 (Oxford: Oxford University Press, 1977), pp. 64-87.

58. Both of these texts are collected in: A. Gasté, La Querelle du Cid (Genève: Slatkine Reprints, 1970).

59. Georges de Scudéry, <u>Observations sur Le Cid</u>, cited in Gasté, p. 75.

60. In the original version of <u>Le Cid</u>, the one Scudéry criticized (1637), the marriage between Chimène and Rodrigue seemed certain, whereas in the editions from 1648 onward, Corneille modified his text and made the marriage between Chimène and Rodrigue much more ambigious. It is believed that Corneille did this as a result of the criticism of his adversaries (both Scudéry and Chapelain).

61. Herbert Fogel states that, "The question of morality, the observance of the social code, and the three unities, all have one important function in dramatic art: their purpose is to render a play plausible. Verisimilitude becomes, therefore, a principal aim of the classical doctrine. In the seventeenth century a literary work was apt to be judged immoral if it violated the rules of <u>bon goût</u> and <u>bienséance</u>. Corneille's plays were often criticized on the ground that they were immoral, according to the conventions, and therefore incredible. Scudéry, for example, violently criticized <u>le Cid</u> because he found Chimène's willingness to marry her father's murderer both improbable and shocking: . . ." (<u>The Criticism of Cornelian Tragedy</u>. New York: Exposition Press, 1967), p. 18.

62. Milorad R. Margitič, "Corneille Un Humaniste Intégral," <u>Papers on French Seventeenth Century Literature</u>, No. 8 (Winter, 1977-78), p. 153.

63. Scudéry, p. 77.

64. Scudéry, p. 80.

65. Georges de Scudéry, <u>Observations sur le Cid</u>, p. 80.

66. Scudéry, p. 82.

67. Scudéry, p. 89.

68. Scudéry, p. 94.

69. From Pierre Corneille's "Lettre apologetique" to Georges de Scudéry, as quoted by Charles Marty-Laveaux in his "Notice" of <u>Oeuvres de</u>

Pierre Corneille, Vol. III (Paris: Hachette,
1862), p. 15.

70. Herbert Fogel emphasizes the similarities between
     Scudéry and Chapelain, "While Chapelain refuted
     many of Scudéry's criticisms, he like Scudéry,
     judged the play from the point of view of
     bienséance and verisimilitude; as a result he
     supported Scudéry's objection that le Cid
     violated accepted social ethics . . ." (The
     Criticism of Cornelian Tragedy.   New York:
     Exposition Press, 1967), p. 19.

71. Jean Chapelain, Les Sentimens de l'Académie
     Françoise sur la Tragi-Comedie Du Cid, cited in
     Gasté, p. 21.

72. Chapelain, p. 30.

73. Chapelain, pp. 36-7.

74. Chapelain, pp. 37-8.

75. Chapelain, p. 40.

76. Chapelain, p. 62.

77. Georges Couton, Corneille (Paris: Hatier, 1958),
     p. 48.

CHAPTER I

THE CREATION OF A FEMALE ETHIC

The unique characteristic of a female ethic, as practiced by Cornelian heroines, is its self-imposed nature. Heroines such as Chimène, Camille, Sabine, Emilie and Pauline reject the dominant male ethic and the public/private split in their lives as a result of unbearable wrongs suffered by them.[78] Their position is one of forced dependency in a patriarchal world, where men and women are in strong opposition to each other.[79] This opposition is centered on male ethics, which are usually defended by the males in the play, and opposed by the females. Cornelian heroines refuse to remain silent and they choose to combat the inhumanity present in a male ethic that is directly responsible for the loss of one of their loved ones.

The female ethic, unlike the male ethic, is not abstract or transcendent. It is an ethic based on what we will find to be female values in the heroines. It will be shown that no outward political or social force demands an action-oriented response from the heroines for wrongs suffered. In fact, because of the constraints imposed upon them by the "bienséances" regarding socially acceptable male/female behavior, direct action is not an available possibility.[80] Cornelian heroines were judged immoral, in their time, because their behavior violated the "bienséances": that which was expected of their sex by society. They choose to act after they have been provoked by some murderous act or some violation of their natural feelings. Their choice to act for themselves, even though a male character will perform the physical act for them, is self-imposed. Society would expect females to remain impassive with regard to male acts of violence committed in the public domain, the male political arena, when the well-being of their own domain, the private one, is violated by the dictates of the male ethic. The image of woman as strong and self-determining, in Corneille's tragedies, was judged immoral and aberrant by society; however, it cannot be denied that Corneille's heroines reflect the growing tradition of the "femme forte,"[81] and that his heroines are creating a self-imposed ethic, which corresponds to that tradition of female heroic behavior.

There are two steps in what is called the creation of a female ethic. The first is, the overt

33

and unquestionable rejection of the dominant male
ethic on the basis of brutality, injustice or the
murder of a loved one. The second is the rejection of
the public/private split. This split, imposed on
women in a patriarchal society, relegates their
activity to the private domain, and forbids their
participation in the political activities of the
public domain. Cornelian heroines reject this split
and choose to act.

After these two steps are examined, it will be
possible to focus on and evaluate the different
qualities present in Corneille's heroines. The
discernment and appreciation of the heroines'
qualities will be the third stage in the process which
is called the creation of a female ethic.

Rejection of Male Ethics

Before we focus on Chimène's rejection of male
ethics in Le Cid, it is necessary to state that in a
feminist critique of a heroine in the theater, the
fact that Chimène, and all the heroines to be studied
here, represent a female character created during the
seventeenth century, is inseparable from the
socio-political reality of being a woman during that
century;

> Comme la femme au 17e siècle,
> l'héroïne cornélienne vit dans un monde
> mâle et patriarchal. Le pouvoir
> socio-politique et l'autorité morale y
> sont du côté du héros en général et du
> père en particulier (viennent
> immédiatement à l'esprit don Diègue,
> Horace, Auguste, Sévère et Polyeucte).
> D'autre part, la preuve suprême du
> Personnage, l'action directe, voire
> même l'épreuve de force, n'est à la
> portée que du héros. . . . Même lorsque
> l'autorité ne se manifeste que
> verbalement, la parole de l'héroïne n'a
> guère autant de poids que celle du
> héros. . . .
> Cela fait que l'héroïne est
> relativement limitée dans ses ambitions
> concrètes, comme dans le choix des
> moyens.[82]

Chimène is a heroine representing the female sex of
her time with all the strictures and limits imposed

34

upon her by seventeenth century society. In his recent book on Corneille, Claude Abraham also stresses the socio-political context of Chimène as a female character: "Limited physically as a woman in a man's world, Chimène refuses to allow her conduct to be guided by these limitations."[83] It is Chimène's refusal to remain within the confines of these limitatons on her sex that renders her, and the other Cornelian heroines in this study, unique heroines in seventeenth century theater. It is because of this refusal that Chimène is a strong image of woman as a self-determining character.

At the beginning of the play, Chimène is perceived as a heroine in a position of forced dependency. She awaits the order of her father, who has the power to determine her fate. Chimène is fearful that her father's choice of a husband for her will not correspond to her own wishes:

> Dis-moi donc, je te prie, une seconde fois
> Ce qui te fait juger qu'il approuve mon choix:
> Apprends-moi de nouveau quel espoir j'en dois prendre;
> (Acte I, Scène i, 17-19)

Chimène is dependent on Elvire, her confidante, for news from her father: "En outre, ne pouvant pas faire d'action directe (par manque de 'bras' ou par 'bienséance'), n'agissant le plus souvent que par l'entremise d'autrui, l'héroine est dependante. . . ."[84] Chimène must act through Elvire so that she does not interfere with the absoluteness of "l'ordre d'un père."

The dominant values in the play are those of the male. Chimène must bow to parental authority because she is forced to do so. Her desires are secondary to those of her father, Le Comte. His choice of a suitable husband for her is based on a male military ethic (Acte i, Scène i, 29-37). Through his daughter's marriage, Le Comte will be able to assure the continued presence of illustrious warriors in his family. Since Chimène's desires and needs are ignored, she becomes a mere pawn in a male ethic that is concerned with its own preservation.

Although Elvire assures Chimène that the man she loves, Rodrigue, will be her father's choice for her husband, she cannot accept this happiness:

> Il semble toutefois que mon âme
> troublée:
> Refuse cette joie, et s'en trouve
> accablée:
> Un moment donne au sort des visages
> divers
> Et dans ce grand bonheur je crains un
> grand revers.
> (Acte I, Scène i, 53-56)

Chimène refuses to accept Elvire's reassurances and
also those of L'Infante:

> Mon coeur outré d'ennuis n'ose rien
> espérer.
> Un orage si prompt que trouble une
> bonace
> D'un naufrage certain nous porte la
> menace:
> Je n'en saurais douter, je péris dans
> le port.
> (Acte II, Scène iii, 448-51)

Chimène has learned of the dispute between her father
and Don Diègue and she senses that something
irreparable has happened. She evokes the image of a
shipwreck which indicates that she has abandoned her
hopes for happiness.

Chimène, with the knowledge of her father's
dispute with Don Diègue, curses her misfortune:
"Maudite ambition, détestable manie, / Dont les plus
généreux souffrent la tyrannie!" (Acte II, Scène iii,
457-58). It is "ambition" that has destroyed her
chances for happiness. Maria Tastevin stresses
Chimène's awareness of her father's values:

> Chimène maudit l'ambition, cette
> "détestable manie," cause de tous ses
> maux. Mais, en vraie fille de
> chevalier, elle comprend pourtant qu'on
> ne peut faillir aux exigences de
> l'honneur. Elle le comprend même trop
> bien pour espérer qu'un accommodement
> finisse la querelle.[85]

And also, Chimène forsees the suffering ahead:
"Honneur impitoyable à mes plus chers désirs, / Que tu
vas me coûter de pleurs et de soupirs!" (Acte II,

Scène iii, 459-60). She is all too familiar with her
father, his values and "points d'honneur": "Les
accommodements ne font rien en ce point: / De si
mortels affronts ne se reparent point" (Acte II, Scène
iii, 467-68). We can infer from these lines that
Chimène fully understands the workings of the male
ethic. She is in the unfortunate position, however,
of waiting for news of the outcome of the dispute:

> Don Diègue est trop altier, et je
> connois mon père.
> Je sens couler des pleurs que je veux
> retenir;
> Le passé me tourmente, et je crains
> l'avenir.
> (Acte II, Scène iii, 478-80)

Chimène is certain that the outcome of this dispute
will cause her much suffering.

Chimène's knowledge of the male ethic also
applies to her understanding of Rodrigue. She knows
that Rodrigue, in his father's defense, will opt for
action that will repair his honor: ". . . Rodrigue
jeune et inconnu encore, mais qui saura faire son
devoir, et dont elle devine, espère et redoute la
vaillance héroïque."[86] Chimène is aware that
Rodrigue, despite his youth, is courageous and only
needs an opportunity to prove it: "Rodrigue a du
courage. . . . / Les hommes valeureux le sont du
premier coup" (Acte II, Scène iii, 482-83). Chimène
understands the nature of the conflict between Don
Diègue and her father, and she knows that her
happiness is doomed because of Rodrigue's inevitable
choice:

> S'il ne m'obéit point, quel comble à
> mon ennui!
> Et s'il peut m'obéir, que dira-t-on de
> lui?
> Etant né ce qu'il est, souffrir un tel
> outrage!
> (Acte II, Scène iii, 487-89)

Rodrigue will respond to the male ethic of honor and
he will place his love for Chimène in a secondary
position.

Once her father is dead, Chimène rushes to the
king's chambers to seek revenge for her father's
death: "Chimène à vos genoux apporte sa douleur; /

Elle vient toute en pleurs vous demander justice"
(Acte II, Scène viii, 659-60). She espouses the male
ethic, and in its own terms, she demands that the
violence committed against her father be punished with
violence:

> Enfin mon père est mort, j'en demande
> vengeance,
> . . . .
> Vous perdez en la mort d'un homme de
> son rang
> Vengez-la par une autre, et le sang par
> le sang.
>   (Acte II, Scène viii, 689; 691-92)

Chimène wants vengeance, as is evident from her bold
declaration: "Son sang sur la poussière écrivoit mon
devoir" (Acte II, Scène viii, 676). She also
demonstrates that she sees her possibilities for
seeking vengeance as equivalent to those of Rodrigue.
Chimène's legitimate right for vengeance is delayed by
the king when he asks her to calm her anger: "Prends
du repos, ma fille, et calme tes douleurs" (Acte II,
Scène viii, 739), and to rest. Chimène persists,
nonetheless, and confronts the king: "M'ordonner du
repos, c'est croître mes malheurs" (Acte ii, Scène
viii, 740), with her resistance to his order. She
will not permit the king to brush her aside or ignore
her; she will persist in her intention to seek
vengeance despite her love for Rodrigue. She knows
what she must do: "Chimène n'hésite pas sur la
conduite à tenir. Son père est mort, elle poursuivra
le meurtrier."[87] Chimène stated her case against
Rodrigue to the king, and he dismissed her from his
court and ordered her back into the seclusion of her
home.

It has already been shown that Chimène knows the
male ethic, its military values and its brutality, and
the suffering it has caused her. After Rodrigue has
responded to the demands of his honor, he begins his
pursuit of Chimène (Acte III, Scène iv). He has
forced his way into Chimene's house (Acte III, Scène
i), hidden himself so that he could spy on Chimène,
and when he reveals his presence to her, he presses
the possibility of more violence on her: "N'épargnez
point mon sang: goûtez sans résistance / La douceur
de ma perte et de votre vengeance" (Acte III, Scène
iv, 853-54). Rodrigue is cruel in his pursuit of her:

38

> Rodrigue a vraiment bien de la
> cruauté en demandant à une aussi tendre
> amante de le tuer elle-même
> . . . .
> mais il sait si bien que Chimène ne
> voudra pas le tuer! Il ne peut douter
> de son amour, il a surpris sa
> conversation avec Elvire et il a
> patiemment attendu, avant de se
> montrer, d'être bien fixé sur ses
> sentiments.[88]

And as Tastevin points out, he waits for an opportune
moment before he reveals his presence to Chimène.
Nadal's view of Rodrigue as Chimène's torturer also
seems accurate. Even though Chimène almost faints
from the shock of this abrupt intrusion: "Hélas! . .
. Je me meurs. . . . / Va, laisse-moi mourir" (Acte
III, Scène iv, 855-56), Rodrigue persists and demands
to be heard: "Quatre mots seulement: / Après ne me
reponds qu'avecque cette épée" (Acte III, Scène iv,
856-57). Rodrigue again insists that Chimène kill him
despite her many protests against this: "Sauve ta
renommée en me faisant mourir" (Acte III, Scène iv,
968).

Rodrigue violates Chimène's desire to be heroic
on her own terms through the means that are accessible
to her. Chimène refuses to kill Rodrigue in cold
blood, and she reveals that she has her own plan for
seeking vengeance against him:

> Elle éclate bien mieux en te laissant
> la vie
> Et je veux que la voix de la plus noire
> envie
> Elève au ciel ma gloire et plaigne mes
> ennuis,
> Sachant que je t'adore et que je te
> poursuis.
> (Acte III, Scène iv, 969-72)

She will not allow Rodrigue to compromise her honor by
his presence in her house or by his entreaties.
Despite his relentless pursuit of her, she will remain
firm in her intentions to seek vengeance:

> Malgré des feux si beaux, qui troublent
> ma colère,
> Je ferai mon possible à bien venger mon
> père;

> Mais malgré la rigueur d'un si cruel
> devoir,
> Mon unique souhait est de ne rien
> pouvoir.
> (Acte III, Scène iv, 981-84)

Nothing has changed. Chimène will continue to seek vengeance for her father's death; however, she does reveal that the rigors of the male ethic, in this case duty, in no way inspire her.

The difficulty of Chimène's struggle stems from the fact that it is self-imposed. There is no ethic that supports her as a woman who wishes to assume an active role. Chimène's ambition is similar to Rodrigue's: she wishes to defend her honor through vengeance; however, the fact that she is female limits her possibilities:

> Mêmes en tant qu'espèce, nourrissant
> des désirs et aspirations identiques,
> ils (héros et héroïnes) diffèrent par
> leurs conditions socio-politiques,
> donc, par leurs ambitions et espoirs
> concrets: leur identité est d'ordre
> anthropologique, leurs différences sont
> d'ordre historique.[89]

Again, the socio-political difference between the hero and heroine is stressed. Despite the limitations imposed upon her, Chimène will continue to pursue Rodrigue:

> Chimène sent trop son devoir pour
> se contenter de pleurer son père en
> silence; elle sait qu'elle a quelque
> chose à faire, elle veut agir et elle
> en a l'illusion en s'agitant. . . . La
> jeune fille veut tranquilliser sa
> conscience en reclamant une fois encore
> la punition du meurtrier.[90]

Chimène is too energetic and angry a heroine to be silenced.

Although Chimène rejects the violence that is the foundation of the male ethic, she has no other alternative but the duel to satisfy her honor. She names the terms that she approves of:

40

> Puis que vous refusez la justice à mes
> larmes
> Sire, permettez-moi de recourir aux
> armes; . . .
> J'épouse le vainqueur, si Rodrigue est
> puni.

that will help her get some action against Rodrigue.
Now that the king has heard Chimène's demands, she
returns to her house (Acte V, Scène i), and is at last
able to rest:

> Rentrée chez elle, la jeune fille
> goûte enfin, pour la première fois
> depuis la mort de son père, un repos
> relatif. Le roi a prononcé, le combat
> aura lieu, Rodrigue triomphera et elle
> sera probablement <u>forcée</u> de
> l'épouser.[91]

Tastevin's emphasis on the forced nature of Chimène's
probable marriage to Rodrigue, is in keeping with the
fact that Chimène, in order to get action against
Rodrigue, was forced to offer herself as the prize of
this duel.

Chimène is painfully aware of her predicament:
she cannot win no matter what she does, and it is
difficult for her to validate her honor because she
has not been able to act for herself:

> A deux rivaux pour moi je fais prendre
> les armes
> Le plus heureux succès me coûtera des
> larmes;
> Et quoi qu'en ma faveur en ordonne le
> sort,
> Mon père est sans vengeance, ou mon
> amant est mort.
> (Acte V, Scène iv, 1649-52)

It is clear that she rejects the male ethic, when she
wishes for the impossible in a world dominated by an
ethic of violence: "Termine ce combat sans aucun
avantage, / Sans faire aucun des deux ni vaincu ni
vainqueur" (Acte V, Scène iv, 1666-67). Chimène also
resists male authority and declares that she will not
be forced to comply with it:

> Quand il sera vainqueur, crois-tu que
> je me rende?

41

Mon devoir est trop fort, et ma perte
trop grande;
Et ce n'est pas assez pour leur faire
la loi,
Que celle du combat et le vouloir du
Roi.
Il peut vaincre don Sanche avec fort
peu de peine,
Mais non pas avec lui la gloire de
Chimène;
Et quoi qu'à sa victoire un monarque
ait promis,
Mon honneur lui fera mille autres
ennemis.
                    (Acte V, Scène iv, 1677-84)

Even after Rodrigue has won the duel, Chimène refuses
to be subjected to an exchange between two men: "Si
Rodrigue a l'Etat devient si nécessaire, / De ce qu'il
fait pour vous dois-je être le salaire" (Acte V, Scène
vii, 1809-10). Why should Chimène allow herself to be
used as a payment for Rodrigue's services to the king?
Chimène resists and rejects the king's authority by
bargaining for more time before she is forced to marry
Rodrigue: "Prends un an, si tu veux, pour essuyer tes
larmes / Rodrigue, cependant il faut prendre les
armes" (Acte V, Scène vii, 1821-22). She has shown
her resistance to the male ethic throughout the play.
At the dénouement of the play, she rejects the male
ethic by opposing male authority and by refusing to
marry Rodrigue.

From the beginning of <u>Horace</u>,[92] an extreme and
rigid polarisation between the sexes is present. Male
and female seem to be at war with each other. Maria
Tastevin refers to this male/female conflict in terms
of a duel:

> C'est le duel éternel des sexes, la
> lutte entre la femme prête en se
> sacrifiant toute à sa passion à y
> sacrifier le monde avec elle, et
> l'homme qui, même épris profondément,
> place en dehors de son amour les
> principes de sa conduite et la fin de
> son action.[93]

while Mauron stresses that the separation between male
and female is a constant in Corneille's theater: "La
faille continue séparant nos deux groupes, selon un
axe horizontal, correspond bien à cette rupture du

42

couple qui est une constante du théâtre cornélien."[94]
Abraham considers the women in Horace subordinate
because of their sex: "Thus Sabine and Camille, as
women, must suffer in the world of men."[95]   And
Doubrovsky, when speaking of Act II of Horace,
emphasizes the confrontation between male and female
values:[96]   It is interesting to note that several
critics pinpoint a male/female opposition in a play
that has war as its theme.

Sabine is the first character in Horace who
stresses the brutality of Roman politics and states
her opposition to war:

> Que les Dieux t'ont permis l'empire de
> la terre,
> Et que tu n'en peux voir l'effet que
> par la guerre: . . . .
> Albe est ton origine: arrête, et
> considère
> Que tu portes le fer dans le sien de ta
> mère.
> (Acte I, Scène i, 43-44; 55-56)

Sabine cannot separate the idea of war from those she
loves: "At the play's beginning the women couched
their opposition to the war in personal terms: they
feared the death of their loved ones."[97]   She compares
the denial of her Alban roots to matricide, and she is
aware that she is unable to ignore her natural
feelings. Nadal has this to add concerning Sabine's
inability to forget her roots and origins:

> Albaine de naissance, mais Romaine par
> son mariage, elle devrait prendre le
> parti des Romains, haïr les ennemis de
> Rome; c'est ce qu'elle ne peut.[98]

Sabine rejects her Roman identity because in her mind
being Roman is equated with brutality and war:
"J'aurois pour mon pays une cruelle haine, / Si je
pouvois encore être toute Romaine" (Acte I, Scène i,
83-84). She is repelled by her Roman identity and
Roman values which are associated with hatred and war.

Camille, like Chimène, is in a position of total
dependence on her father's authority. Yet, in
Camille's case, her marriage has been approved before
the beginning of the play. When referring to
Shakespearian heroines, Eva Figes emphasizes the
forced dependency of a daughter on her father, and on

43

his choice of a marriage partner: "In a patriarchal society a daughter's obedience to her father is absolute. Her father makes the ultimate decision as to whom she shall marry, and as a result many dramas hinge on the fact."[99] Even though Camille's husband has been chosen for her, the fact that Rome will wage war against Alba makes her future happiness highly doubtful. Camille expresses this violent reversal in her fate and Curiace's:

> Ce jour nous fut propice et funeste à
> la fois:
> Unissant nos maisons, il désunit nos
> rois;
> Un même instant conclut notre hymen et
> la guerre,
> Fit naître notre espoir et le jeta par
> terre,
> Nous ôta tout, sitôt qu'il nous eut
> tout promis,
> Et nous faisant amants, il nous fit
> ennemis.
>   (Acte I, Scène ii, 173-78)

The fact that war is directly responsible for the total reversal of Camille's fortune helps us understand her anger throughout the play.

Camille is opposed to this war and she makes it clear that she cannot accept any man who has shed blood in war like her husband. Camille arrives at this decision before Curiace appears in her home:

> Soit que Rome y succombe ou qu'Albe ait
> le dessous,
> Cher amant, n'attends plus d'être un
> jour mon époux;
> Jamais, jamais ce nom ne sera pour un
> homme
> Qui soit ou le vainqueur, ou l'esclave
> de Rome.
>   (Acte I, Scène ii, 229-32)

With respect to this decision, Camille and Sabine resemble each other in wanting a love that is not soiled by blood: ". . . the love of Sabine and Camille is deeply moral since it champions human life above the vagaries of political expediency."[100] The preservation of human life is far more important to Camille and Sabine than any political goal.

44

Like Rodrigue, Curiace appears unexpectedly in
Camille's house. This visit is not felt to be a
shocking violation of Camille's privacy, as was the
case with Rodrigue's visit, because no blood has been
shed, which is Curiace's claim (Acte I, Scène iii,
235-40). Yet, Camille is disturbed by Curiace's entry
into her house because she fears her father's
authority if he discovers Curiace:

> Mais as-tu vu mon père, et peut-il
> endurer
> Qu'ainsi dans sa maison tu t'oses
> retirer?
> Ne préfère-t-il point l'Etat à sa
> famille?
> Ne regarde-t-il point Rome plus que sa
> fille?
>
> (Acte I, Scène iii, 253-56)

Camille suspects that her father treasures the State
and Rome over his family, which violates her love for
the family and human life. Curiace's visit is cruel
because Camille is misled by him into believing that
he too values love and the preservation of human life
over political goals achieved through war. This is
not to say that Camille is not patriotic, or capable
of such feelings:

> Les liens qui la retiennent à la
> communauté familiale et sociale sont
> donc solides; Camille est la jeune
> fille d'un sang, d'un milieu, d'un
> culte particuliers. Elle prend part
> aux dangers, aux espérances de ses
> frères et de la cité.[101]

but, above all else, she values life, and is
absolutely opposed to war.

When Camille first sees her brother, Horace, he
warns her to accept the victor of the duel no matter
who he may be:

> Armez-vous de constance, et
> montrez-vous ma soeur;
> Et si par mon trépas il retourne
> vainqueur,
> Ne le recevez point en meurtrier d'un
> frère,
> Mais en homme d'honneur qui fait ce
> qu'il doit faire, ...

45

> Comme si je vivois, achevez l'hyménée;
> Mais si ce fer aussi tranche sa
> destinée,
> Faites à ma victoire un pareil
> traitement:
> Ne me reprochez point la mort de votre
> amant.
> Vos larmes vont couler, et votre coeur
> se presse.
> Consumez avec lui toute cette
> foiblesse,
> . . . .
> Mais après le combat ne pensez plus au
> mort.
> (Acte II, Scène iv, 517-20; 523-28;
> 530)

We must remember that Camille has just learned of a harsh reversal in her fortune: Curiace was chosen to fight. Without having time to react to the cruelty of this misfortune, Horace warns his sister in rigid and brutal terms that she essentially must overcome her feelings. "Camille must arm herself with constancy which is: ". . . the outward control of the passions, while suffering . . . internal revolt. . . ."[102] Camille's tears, if Curiace dies, must be suppressed. Horace has given his warning without letting Camille react; he has not taken into account her values which oppose the male war ethic, and he expects her to suppress all of her natural feelings for human life. Camille cannot speak abstractly of human life and death as Horace can:

> In Horace women express themselves in
> very concrete and human terms. . . .
> For them the war between Rome and Alba
> is not simply a confrontation between
> two countries, but between men that
> they love, and in such a struggle there
> can be no triumphs, only the death of
> loved ones and a lingering hatred for
> those who survive. . . .[103]

Both Camille and Sabine are not capable of being abstract about the possible loss of their husbands or lovers. They view war as an odious destroyer of life. Camille is aware of the consequences of war and she warns that if Curiace dies, she must join him in death:

> Il faut bien que je pleure:
> Mon insensible amant ordonne que je meure;
> Et quand l'hymen pour nous allume son flambeau,
> Il l'éteint de sa main pour m'ouvrir le tombeau.
> Ce coeur impitoyable à ma perte s'obstine,
> Et dit qu'il m'aime encore alors qu'il m'assassine.
> (Acte II, Scène v, 572-76)

Camille rejects the cruelty of the male ethic and threatens to retaliate if Curiace is murdered. For her, the male ethic is synonymous with inhuman demands and brutality. The women in <u>Horace</u> "are opposed to the harsh strictures and inhuman codes of men (described by them as 'brutalité'). . . ."[104]

When Camille is finally able to release her long frustrated pain and anger, after Curiace's death, she in effect attempts to strip herself of male values:

> Dégénérons, mon coeur, d'un si vertueux père;
> Soyons indigne soeur d'un si généreux frère:
> C'est gloire de passer pour un coeur abattu,
> Quand la brutalité fait la haute vertu.
> Eclatez, mes douleurs: à quoi bon vous contraindre?
> Quand on a tout perdu, que sauroit-on plus craindre?
> (Acte IV, Scène iv, 1239-44)

Camille has nothing to lose and she intends to take action against an insane world: "In such a universe the only recourse open to a sane person is to reject these values completely and to become a degenerate in society's eyes in order to preserve a modicum of humanity."[105] There is no reason why Camille should restrain her anger which has been building up for a long time: "Son explosion de colère et de rage est l'aboutissement nécessaire et attendu de la silencieuse fermentaiton de ses idées, du bouillonnement jusque-là contenu de ses émotions."[106] Camille cannot passively accept the wrongs she has suffered. She unleashes her hatred against an ethic that has ruined any chance for happiness in her life.

Tastevin describes the nature of this hatred: "Camille est trop énergique pour s'abîmer dans une tristesse inerte et résignée. Sa passion frustrée de son objet, ses regrets irrités, se transforment en une haine violente, avide de représailles."[107]

Horace considers Camille a threatening Roman enemy and he kills her and curses her: "Va dedans les enfers plaindre ton Curiace" (Acte IV, Scène v, 1320). The conflict between them seems to be the most central in the play: ". . . chacun voit en l'autre son pire adversaire: celui qui poursuit jusqu'à la mort ce qu'il idolâtre jusqu'à l'immolation. Horace l'emporte parce qu'il a la force physique brutale; mais Camille est moralement invaincue."[108] Horace's murder of Camille, which as Tastevin emphasizes is totally unequal, can be interpreted as an attempt to eradicate female values which cannot coexist in a world dominated by a brutal male ethic. Yet, morally, Camille is invincible because her values uphold the preservation of human life. As a result, her criticism of the violence of the male ethic remains a powerful result of the dénouement:

> Thus his great tragedies contain an implicit critique of this ideal as the same time as they praise fulsomely those who pursue it. In Horace the women question gloire, and although by the fifth act these critics are either dead (Camille) or rendered ineffective (Sabine), their arguments linger with the audience and pervade the play's final moments.[109]

The male ethic is condemned by Camille which includes its ideals ("gloire," for example), and its political goals. The consequence of her rejection of male ethics is a violent death for she and Horace cannot coexist in the same world.

When Emilie sees Auguste before her eyes, her only desire is to kill him (Acte I, Scène i, 9-16), and seek vengeance for her father's murder. Emilie questions the validity of good deeds or munificence that come from an unscrupulous dictator (Acte I, Scène ii, 73-82). She cannot separate Octave's bloody past from the calmer present of the Roman emperor, Auguste:

> Et Emilie, les yeux fixés avec obstination sur le passé, Emilie qui

48

dans Auguste ne considérait jamais qu'Octave, a vu dans son ennemi un ambitieux sans scrupules, un criminel sans remords, un tyran oppresseur de la Patrie.[110]

Emilie cannot accept Auguste as the rightful emperor of Rome, because he rose to power through many acts of violence; she cannot think in abstract terms about the many murders that put Auguste on the throne. Her father was one of those who was murdered and she has never forgiven Auguste for that loss in her life. Emilie can only view his munificence ("les bienfaits") as acts that emanate from an impure source: ". . . elle veut s'en libérer et s'affirmer, elle et Cinna, contre les bienfaits impurs de l'empereur."[111] She disregards Auguste's favors towards her throughout the years. During that time, Emilie's desire to seek revenge for her father's death has grown stronger: "Emilie ne songe qu'à venger un père et refuse de mettre en compte les bienfaits."[112] In fact, Emilie has been using the gifts, bestowed upon her by Auguste, to serve her needs in a conspiracy which she initiated (Acte I, Scène ii, 79-84). Emilie does not value favors that come from a tyrant who used Machiavellian means to gain his power.[113] In other words, Emilie rejects the male ethic of "la loi du plus fort."

Emilie remains independent and firmly opposed to Auguste's munificence, while Cinna is influenced and swayed by it. He even tries to convince Emilie to relinquish all vengeance against Auguste (Acte III, Scène iv). Emilie, however, is only insulted by Auguste's favors, and continues to assert her independence from them: "Mais ce que Cinna considère comme un bienfait suprême est bien plutôt pour Emilie une suprême insulte: Auguste se permet de disposer d'elle comme si elle lui appartenait."[114] Emilie belongs to no one, and she rejects any favor that comes from a man who seized power over Rome through repeated violence and unscrupulous means.

Much later in the play, when Auguste and Emilie confront each other for the first time, Auguste implores Emilie: "O ma fille est-ce là le prix de mes bienfaits?" (Acte V, Scène ii, 1595), and Emilie bluntly replies: "Ceux de mon père en vous firent mêmes effets" (Acte V, Scène ii, 1596). It is apparent that Emilie remains firm in her rejection of Auguste's "bienfaits." His clemency comes as a surprise to Emilie, in what is Auguste's conversion and not Emilie's.[115] It appears that Emilie accepts Auguste's clemency after she believes that she has satisfied her desire to avenge her father's death (Acte V, Scène ii, 1645-56). As late as Act V, Scene II, Emilie remains unchanged; she confronts Auguste with the difference between her ambition and his:

> Et vous m'avez au crime enseigné le chemin:
> Le mien d'avec le vôtre en ce point seul diffère,
> Que votre ambition s'est immolé mon père,

The underlined words (emphasis mine) imply Auguste's conversion.

> Et qu'un juste courroux, dont je me sens brûler,
> A son sang innocent vouloit vous immoler.
>
> (Acte V, Scène ii, 1600-4)

Auguste has blood on his hands, whereas Emilie, who did not succeed in killing Auguste, has shed no blood. Emilie accepts Auguste's clemency as a means to avoid further bloodshed. She openly declared her desire to kill Auguste: ". . . car elle ne croit pas que le cruel Octave puisse avoir de la clémence. . . ."[116] Emilie rejected Auguste's Machiavellian ethic by rejecting his past munificence, which had a false foundation, and was based on violent acts. It seems likely that she accepts Auguste's clemency because she sees his conversion as an end to future bloodshed.

Pauline is a heroine who inhabits an all-male world. This world of male values determines her fate.[117] Her primary relationships revolve around three men: her father, Félix; her husband, Polyeucte; and her former suitor, Sévère. If we return to the notion of forced dependency, we find Pauline, like the other tragic heroines in this study, circumventing this position of forced dependency and being self-determining in whatever way possible. Pauline's obedience to Félix is not blind and unquestioning. She opposes him especially when his demands are unreasonable and against her feelings.

Pauline is a complex heroine[118] who is self-conscious, and aware that she is very important

to the fate of her country: "In a word the heroines
of Corneille one and all are thoroughly tinctured with
politics."[119] We will see that her marriage is
inextricable from the political interest of the play,
and that Félix urges her to obey him in order to
further his political career. Her father insists that
she obey him no matter what the cost may be:

> Dans la tragédie, les volontés du père
> deviendront des impératifs d'honneur ou
> d'Etat, les soucis d'argent se mueront
> en desseins politiques, mais de toute
> façon l'amour demeurera subordonné. La
> conscience de Corneille et son héros
> tombent d'accord qu'il doit en être
> ainsi, que l'ordre du monde l'exige.[120]

The underlined portion (emphasis mine), stresses that
Pauline, like other Cornelian heroines, functions in a
patriarchal world where her interests must remain
subordinate. Mauron's interesting theories will be
pursued further when we examine Pauline's fate at the
end of the play.

Pauline's resistance to and eventual rejection of
parental authority represents her rejection of male
ethics. This rejection is a result of Pauline's
perception of Félix's unreasonable demands. Since
Pauline's refusal to obey is gradual, we will examine
the situation which leads to her rejection of parental
authority.

Félix, as Pauline's father, has absolute power
over the choice of her marriage partner. Pauline's
preferences and desires need not be taken into
account. Her eventual marriage to Polyeucte is a
forced marriage,[121] which is against her will, and
against her real desire to have married Sévère. Félix
forced her into a political marriage, of which she
laments to her confidante:

> Le reste, tu le sais: mon abord en ces
> lieux
> Me fit voir Polyeucte, et je plus à ses
> yeux;
> Et comme il est ici chef de la
> noblesse,
> Mon père fut ravi qu'il me prît pour
> maîtresse,
> Et par son alliance il se crut assuré
> D'être   plus   redoutable   et   plus

considéré:

>   Il approuva sa flamme, et conclut
>   l'hyménée;
>   (Acte I, Scène iii, 207-13)

Despite the lack of personal choice, Pauline's obedience is not blind. She tells Stratonice, her confidante, that she made it clear to her lover, Sévère, that she was deeply hurt by her father's decision:

>   Il possédoit mon coeur, mes desirs, ma
>   pensée:
>   Je ne lui cachois point combien j'étois
>   blessée:
>   Nous soupirions ensemble, et pleurions
>   nos malheurs;
>   Mais au lieu d'espérance, il n'avoit
>   que des pleurs;
>   Et malgré des soupirs si doux, si
>   favorables,
>   Mon père et mon devoir étoient
>   inexorables.
>   (Acte I, Scène iii, 197-202)

Pauline did not hide her feelings of hurt and displeasure from Sévère. She also did not obey her father without deep regret. This finding runs counter to several critics' theories on Pauline's obedience. Nadal assumes that Pauline acquiesces: "Pour l'instant elle est docile, obéissante, romanesque, mais sans le courage de l'amour. . . ."[122] Allentuch observes that Pauline is submissive, though not invariably so: ". . . Pauline, at first submissive, later rebels."[123] Tastevin goes a step farther and states that the thought of resistance did not even occur to Pauline:

>   Et lorsque Félix s'est opposé à son
>   mariage, Pauline s'est inclinée.
>   C'était pour elle un axiome que la
>   volonté d'un père ne se discute pas.
>   Elle a souffert, elle a pleuré, mais
>   l'idée de résister ne lui est même pas
>   venue.[124]

Pauline's obedience to Félix is indisputable; however, she is not puppetlike in her obedience. She viewed her father's change of mind as betrayal (Acte I, Scène iii, 195-6), and was deeply hurt when her needs and desires were ignored. She is aware of the sacrifices she had made for Félix: "Enfin je quittai Rome et ce parfait amant, / Pour suivre ici mon père en son gouvernement" (Acte, Scène iii, 202-3). Pauline is also aware that she has rights, and that she can confront Félix with the sacrifices she had made to fulfill her filial duty.

Long after Pauline has agreed to marry Polyeucte, Félix makes new demands. Once it is learned that Sévère is still alive, Félix, who fears Pauline's prophetic dream, forces her to see Sévère. Additional psychological violence will be done to Pauline. Several critics emphasize that Pauline is forced to see Sévère:

> . . . le mouvement de Pauline vers Sévère est non pas un retour inspiré par une tendresse encore vivante ou par le souvenir d'une blessure mal refermée, mais exactement l'exécution d'un ordre, l'accomplissement d'un devoir. Toute la perspective de l'entrevue change si l'on tient compte de cette remarque. Pauline vient trouver Sévère en service commandé.[125]

Tastevin also stresses the forced nature of this encounter: "Elle voudrait éviter Sévère, avoir au moins le temps de se remettre. Et Félix la conjure de parler, dès son arrivée, au tout puissant visiteur."[126]

We can see that Pauline is being pushed to her limits by an unreasonable father and authority figure. In his fear of Sévère's impending visit, Félix thinks only of himself: "O ciel! en quel état ma fortune est réduite!" (Acte I, Scène iv, 317). Félix shows his unreasonable nature when he even blames Pauline for having obeyed him in the past:

> Ah! Pauline, en effet, tu m'as trop obéi;
> Ton courage étoit bon, ton devoir l'a trahi.
> Que ta rébellion m'eût été favorable!
> Qu'elle m'eût garanti d'un état déplorable.
> (Acte I, Scène iv, 331-34)

Félix fears Sévère and asks Pauline to see him and to use his love to manipulate him: "Ménage en ma faveur

53

l'amour qui le possède, / Et d'où provient mon mal fais sortir le remède" (Acte I, Scène iv, 337-38). Pauline is outraged by Félix's requests. She does not want to risk seeing Sévère:

> Moi, moi! que je revoie un si puissant vainqueur,
> Et m'expose à des yeux qui me percent le coeur!
> Mon père, je suis femme et je sais ma foiblesse;
> . . . .
> Je ne le verrai point.
> (Acte I, Scène iv, 339-41; 345)

However, Félix forces her to obey: "Il faut le voir ma fille. / Ou tu trahis ton père et toute ta famille" (Acte I, Scène iv, 349-50). Pauline's obedience is conditional because she has warned Félix of the risks involved. She makes this clear to him: "C'est à moi d'obéir, puisque vous commandez; / Mais voyez les périls où vous me hasardez" (Acte I, Scène iv, 351-52).

As Allentuch has pointed out, Pauline, like the Princesse de Clèves, is a pawn for her parent's ambition:

> Neither chose her mate; both were sacrificial pawns of parental ambitions for status, wealth, or power. Each adopted a solution faithful to the highest demands of the aristocratic conscience. Forced to push aside natural feelings, both pursued a sense of worth in punctilious observance of duty, moral circumspection, and decorous behavior.[127]

Félix reminds her that his fate and hers are in her hands: "Rappelle cependant tes forces étonnées, / Et songe qu'en tes mains tu tiens nos destinées" (Acte I, Scène iv, 361-62). Félix is asking Pauline to ignore her natural feelings. She obeys but does so unwillingly: "Qui, je vais de nouveau dompter mes sentiments, / Pour servir de victime à vos commandements" (Acte I, Scène iv, 363-64). Allentuch perceives these lines as an indication of the true relationship that exists between Pauline and Félix: "Pauline is more direct. She moves from resistance and insult to active rebellion against her egocentric

father."[128]   There is an element of truth in
Allentuch's remarks; however, Pauline and Félix's
relationship is more complex than that of a
victim/executioner, though that relationship is one
aspect of their interaction.

Félix's rigidity and unreasonable nature are
directly responsible for Pauline's eventual rejection
of his authority. Félix is responsible for the
Pauline/Polyeucte match, and yet he never assumes that
responsibility. He expects Pauline to solve their
problems, such as the threat posed by Sévère's
reappearance and Polyeucte's conversion to
Christianity. He lays the burdens of his decisions
and their consequences on his daughter. He even
denies the importance of family ties: "Les Dieux et
l'Empereur sont plus que ma famille" (Acte III, Scène
iii, 930). Pauline recognizes that her father's
behavior is extreme and rigid ("Quel excès de
rigueur!" (Acte III, Scène iii, 927), and that his
vacillations are a sign of his weakness. Lancaster
pinpoints the differences between Pauline and Félix:

> There is a marked contrast between
> Pauline's straightforward nature and
> the self-seeking character of her
> father, the typical politician. Félix
> is by no means altogether evil, but he
> is weak, he has passed his life in an
> atmosphere of intrigue and diplomacy,
> and he is unable to see farther than
> the immediate future, or to understand
> motives that are finer than his own.[129]

Félix no longer represents a stable political system;
and the depiction of his weakness is linked to the
literary technique of inversion of the sexes. Further
mention of inversion will be made later on in the
section on the heroine's qualities.

Félix's overt political opportunism, most often
at Pauline's expense, causes his abrupt treatment of
her: "Allez: n'irritez plus un père qui vous aime, /
Et tâchez d'obtenir votre époux de lui-même" (Acte
III, Scène iv, 985-986). This type of treatment
eventually leads to her confrontation with Félix. She
blames him for joining her fate to Polyeucte's:

> Nos destins, par vos mains rendus
> inséparables,
> Nous doivent rendre heureux ensemble,

ou misérables;
Et vous seriez cruel jusques au dernier
point,
Si vous désunissiez ce que vous avez
joint.
(Acte V, Scène iii, 1627-30)

She reminds him that he is responsible for their
marriage. Pauline finally disobeys him and rebels
against his authority:

Père barbare, achève, achève ton
ouvrage:
. . . .
Joins ta fille à ton gendre; ose: que
tardes-tu?
(Acte V, Scène v, 1719; 1721)

She has rejected Félix after his continual and
increasing abuse: ". . . she too rebels against male
authority, although not until the dénouement of
Polyeucte, when she rejects her father, shown as
repeatedly insensitive to her feelings and moral
aspirations."[130] Although Pauline's rebellion occurs
at the dénouement, Pauline began resisting his orders
as early as Act I, Scene iv.[131]

Pauline's rebellion is complete when she has
converted to Christianity, after she has witnessed
Polyeucte's brutal murder:

Mon époux en mourant m'a laissé ses
lumières;
Son sang, dont tes bourreaux viennent
de me couvrir,
. . . .
Je vois, je sais, je crois, je suis
désabusée:
De ce bienheureux sang tu me vois
baptisée.
(Acte V, Scène v, 1724-25; 1727-28)

Her conversion affirms the fact that she is, "beyond
the reach of external authority."[132] She is finally
untouchable as far as Félix's authority is concerned.
Pauline will disobey him. She asserts that fact with
pride: "Une fois envers toi manquer d'obéissance"
(Acte V, Scène v, 1740). Just as Polyeucte was able
to reject all earthly ambition and rise above any
external authority, Pauline is able to reject male
authority and become immune to it. Allentuch credits

Corneille with the ability to make Pauline's rebellion
comprehensible:

> But in fleshing out her character and
> fitting her into a plot many of whose
> elements were entirely of his own
> devising, he made her comprehensible in
> purely human terms and brought into
> focus her feelings of anger and
> confinement as a woman bandied about by
> men free to dictate her fate.[133]

Once and for all, Pauline has become immune to Félix's
parental authority. She rejects it and rebels against
its irresponsibility.

It is true that men dictate Pauline's fate;
however, she is able to curb this power over her by
voicing her protests. She protested against Félix and
finally made him powerless over her. She also curbed
Polyeucte's power as her husband by resisting his
efforts to determine her fate after his death.
Polyeucte felt it was within his power to give Pauline
to his rival, Sévère:

> Je vous ai fait, Seigneur, une
> incivilité,
> . . . .
> Possesseur d'un tresor dont je n'étois
> pas digne,
> Souffrez avant ma mort que je vous le
> résigne
> (Acte IV, Scène iv, 1297; 1299-1300)

Polyeucte was referring to Pauline when he spoke of
himself as her possessor. Polyeucte summoned Sévère
(Acte IV, Scène iv) in order to permit Sévère to
possess Pauline after his death:

> Just before death, savoring
> thoughts of heaven, he continues
> nonetheless to make extravagant demands
> upon his wife. As if she were
> property, demanding to be liquidated,
> he summons Sévère in her presence and
> tries to bestow her upon him.[134]

Pauline's reaction to this exchange was outrage and
refusal:

Qu'il n'est point aux enfers d'horreurs
que je n'endure,
Plutôt que de souiller une gloire si
pure,
Que d'épouser un homme, après son
triste sort,
Qui de quelque façon soit cause de sa
mort;
Et si vous me croyiez d'une âme si peu
saine,
L'amour que j'eus pour vous tourneroit
toute en haine.
                    (Acte IV, Scène v, 1343-48)

Polyeucte thought that he could give Pauline to
Sévère: "C'est Polyeucte qui disculpe son rival; il
fait plus, il lui cède Pauline."[135] Yet, he did not
envision her refusal. Pauline rejects Polyeucte's
solution to his abandonment of her. She refuses to be
Sévère's wife after Polyeucte's death; she refuses to
permit them to treat her as if she were property.

Rejection of the Public/Private Split

Chimène is a heroine whose private needs are
always relegated to a secondary position. The public
good, whether it be determined by her father or by the
king, must come before Chimène's private needs and
desires. Chimène is repeatedly forced to accept this;
however, she will be able to modify the absoluteness
of the demands of the public/private split through her
resistance against it.

As the play opens, Chimène is fearful that her
private and personal happiness, which consists of
being permitted to marry the man she loves, will be
threatened. We find Chimène in the privacy of her
home, and in the company of her confidante--her link
to the outside world, and the intermediary between her
and her father. Chimène is in a precarious position
because the only influence she has on her father, the
person who has the power to determine her fate without
her consent, is indirect. Although Le Comte seems to
prefer Rodrigue, Chimène's choice for her future
husband, Chimène believes that her personal happiness
is doomed:

Il semble toutefois que mon âme
troublée:
Refuse cette joie, et s'en trouve
accablée:

58

Un moment donne au sort des visages
divers
Et dans ce grand bonheur je crains un
grand revers.
                    (Acte I, Scène i, 53-6)

because she has learned from Elvire, her confidante,
that Le Comte intends to mix private business, his
daughter's marriage, with public business, the
election of a "gouverneur." Chimène senses that this
will prove disastrous.

One of the most fundamental characteristics of
Chimène's behavior is her awareness of the split
between public and private domains. Chimène is a
character who experiences a severe division between
her public and private selves, based on whether she is
in the public eye or in the privacy of her home. In
the 1648 Avertissement of Le Cid, Corneille emphasizes
the discrepancy in Chimène's behavior based on where
and whom she is with:

C'est, si je ne me trompe, comme
agit Chimène dans mon ouvrage, en
présence du Roi et de l'Infante. je
dis en présence du Roi et de l'Infante,
parce que quand elle est seule, ou avec
sa confidente, ou avec son amant, c'est
une autre chose. Ses moeurs sont
inégalement égales, pour parler en
termes de notre Aristote, et changent
suivant les circonstances des lieux,
des personnes, des temps et des
occasions, en conservant toujours le
même principe.[136]

Chimène is sensitive to the difference in behavior
that is demanded by each domain. It will also be
shown that even with her lover, Chimène maintains her
public reserve until Rodrigue forces her to reveal her
private thoughts.

After Chimène learns of the dispute between Don
Dièize and Le Comte (Acte II, Scène iii), she is aware
that as a woman relegated to the private domain, she
is unable to affect disputes between men in the public
domain. She knows that Rodrigue will be called upon
to defend his father's honor in a duel, and that all
she can do is await the outcome. We have also seen
that from the Stances, the outcome of this duel will
favor Rodrigue's honor and not his love. The opposing

values delineated by Rodrigue fall into two distinct domains: the public and the private. In the public domain are, father and honor, which oppose, mistress and love in the private domain. Even though Rodrigue identified his happiness with Chimène ("ma Chimène"), the values in the public domain far outweigh those in the private domain. Chimène knows that Rodrigue will choose his honor over love.

Once Le Comte is dead, Chimène rushes to the king's palace to demand justice. Chimène describes the scene she saw after the duel and how she witnessed her father's death:

> Sire, mon père est mort; mes yeux ont vu son sang
> Couler à gros bouillons de son généreux flanc;
> . . . .
> J'ai couru sur le lieu, sans force et sans couleur:
> Je l'ai trouvé sans vie.
> . . . .
> Sire, de trop d'honneur ma misère est suivie.
> Je vous l'ai déjà dit, je l'ai trouvé sans vie
> (Acte II, Scène viii, 659-60; 667-68; 673-74)

She emphasizes the violence of the scene she has just seen; she must use her grief to gain the attention of the king. Although Chimène's laments are heard, the king orders her to return to her house: "Don Sanche, remettez Chimène en sa maison / Don Diègue aura ma cour et sa foi pour prison" (Acte II, Scène viii, 735-36). Implicit in the king's order to put Chimène back in her house, is the fact that Chimène has appeared where women are rarely seen: in the king's chambers. Chimène has violated the public/private split in doing so. Order must be restored by placing Chimène back in her home, in the private domain, the one to which she belongs. Also, the fact that Chimène has to be put back ("remettez") in her home by Don Sanche, her appointed escort, indicates that she is a woman who has limited power in the political, public world of men.

Few Cornelian critics have interpreted Act III in light of the fact that Rodrigue's entry into Chimène's house is a _forced_ entry. Rodrigue entered Chimène's

60

house, her only refuge, without her knowledge. It is
with this fact in mind that Act III will be
interpreted, and that the violence committed against
her will be examined.

Both Nadal and Charles Mauron emphasize the
violence of Rodrigue's pursuit of Chimène, in her own
house, during her mourning period:

> Il y a du mepris dans cet acharnement
> de Rodrigue à poursuivre Chimène comme
> une proie; . . . En fait, il y joue le
> rôle de tortionnaire vis-à-vis de sa
> victime, qu'il tourmente jusqu'à ce
> qu'il ait obtenu de sa bouche l'aveu
> qu'elle est vaincue par l'amour.[137]

and: "Il force donc Chimène comme on force une
proie."[138] Rodrigue's pursuit of Chimène is
unrelenting, cruel and sadistic. While Chimène is
still at the king's palace, Rodrigue forces his way
into Chimène's house. Elvire warns him that his
presence is not welcome: "Rodrigue, fuis, de grâce:
ôte-moi de souci" (Acte III, Scène i, 767); however,
Rodrigue ignores Elvire's requests until she must beg
him to think of Chimène's honor: "Du moins, pour son
honneur, Rodrigue, cache-toi" (Acte III, Scène i,
772). Rather than leaving, as Elvire has begged him
to do, Rodrigue's concession is to hide himself in
Chimène's house and spy on her private thoughts. This
illustrates how Chimène is denied the privacy of her
own home. Even though the private domain is the
female realm, it can be violated when it suits the
needs of a male. We shall see how Chimène is subject
to psychological harassment in her own home.

The most significant scene for a "re-vision" and
reinterpretation of Chimène's character is Scene iii
of Act III. Chimène believes that she is finally free
in the privacy of her home with her confidante,
Elvire. She has no way of knowing that Rodrigue is
present. Rodrigue's hidden presence is a violation of
Chimène's private space, and it is a source of
deception. Chimène begins to reveal her most private
thoughts under these circumstances:

> Enfin je me vois libre, et je puis sans
> contrainte
> De mes vives douleurs te faire voir
> l'atteinte;
> Je puis donner passage à mes tristes

soupirs;
Je puis t'ouvrir mon âme et tous mes déplaisirs.
      Mon père est mort, Elvire; et la première épée
Dont s'est armé Rodrigue, a sa trame coupée.
Pleurez, pleurez, mes yeux, et fondez-vous en eau!
La moitié de ma vie a mis l'autre au tombeau,
Et m'oblige à venger, après ce coup funeste,
Celle que je n'ai plus sur celle qui me reste.
                    (Acte III, Scène iii, 793-802)

Chimène is not aware of the irony of her situation since she believes that she is free to express how she really feels:

> Seule avec sa confidente, ou plutôt croyant l'être, Chimène pousse un soupir de soulagement. Elle peut enfin, sans souci de jouer un rôle, s'abandonner à sa douleur, pleurer son père et sa propre infortune.[139]

Tastevin aptly expresses insights that help us understand Chimène's character, particularly when she enters her home and is relieved to express herself without the restraints of the public domain.

It is not surprising that Chimène is extremely shocked when Rodrigue suddenly appears before her, sword in hand, in her house: "Elvire, où sommes-nous, et qu'est-ce que je voi? / Rodrigue en ma maison! Rodrigue devant moi!" (Acte III, Scène iv, 851-852). Tastevin is again penetrating in her analysis of Chimène's reaction:

> Ce Rodrigue, qui occupe tant sa pensée, le voici qui brusquement, paraît à ses yeux. La surprise, l'émotion, la lutte intense et rapide entre deux sentiments contradictoires font presque défaillir Chimène. Son trouble augmente encore à la vue de l'épée de Rodrigue, de cette épée qui évoque de si terribles et sanglants souvenirs.[140]

62

Chimène's right to her private space in the domain that is relegated to the female, the private one, is violated by Rodrigue's unwelcome presence in her house. Instead of Chimène pursuing Rodrigue, he is mercilessly pursuing her until he is satisfied and certain of her love for him:

> Rodrigue poursuit une dialectique qui rassemble les meilleurs arguments destinés à forcer les hésitations de Chimène. Celle-ci se défend pied à pied, répond avec beaucoup de souplesse et de précision, renchérit sur la rigueur de point d'honneur, mais finit par avouer qu'elle ne peut le haïr. Malgré cet aveu, il ne cesse de la tourmenter, de provoquer et de consommer sa ruine morale; enfin il ne la quitte qu'elle n'ait révélé sa pensée la plus intime: souhaiter que la poursuite judiciaire n'aboutisse pas.[141]

Nadal manages to pinpoint the type of dynamic existing between Rodrigue and Chimène, and emphasize how Rodrigue has forced her to reveal her most private thoughts. However, Chimène's moral ruin, does not seem to be a consequence of this visit. Rodrigue might have forced Chimène to express her most private thoughts; yet, her intention to seek vengeance against him has not changed.

As Rodrigue's public reputation as a national hero grows, Chimène's chances to continue pursuing Rodrigue, or to succeed at repairing her honor, become more difficult. L'Infante will inform Chimène of the fact that her private desire for vengeance opposes the public good:

> Rodrigue maintenant est notre unique appui,
> . . . .
> Le Roi même est d'accord de cette vérité,
> Que ton père en lui seul se voit ressuscité;
> . . . .
> Ote-lui ton amour, mais laisse-nous sa vie.
>   (Acte IV, Scène ii, 1176; 1179-80; 1182; 1190)

Rodrigue has become a public hero, and Chimène's revenge is considered a private vendetta that threatens the country with the loss of its protector.

Chimène's right to her privacy during her mourning period will be violated again as Act V begins. Rodrigue's second forced entry into Chimène's house occurs, and it is met with the same shock on Chimène's part: "Quoi! Rodrigue, en plein jour! d'où te vient cette audace? / Va, tu me perds d'honneur; retire-toi, de grâce" (Acte V, Scène i, 1465-66). Chimène begs him to leave but he refuses. As in Act III, Rodrigue's forced presence in Chimène's house facilitates his ability to force her to admit her love for him, and to reveal her most private thoughts. This is the case when Chimène cries: "Sors vainqueur d'un combat dont Chimène est le pris. / Adieu: ce mot lâché me fait rougir de honte" (Acte V, Scène i, 1556-57). Chimène blushes at her own words which shock her sense of modesty and reserve. Once again Rodrigue has violated Chimène's rights in the private domain.

Sabine is the first female character to express the painful divisions caused by the public/private split. In the privacy of her home, accompanied by her confidante, Sabine reveals her true feelings about being Roman through marriage:

> Je suis Romaine, hélas! puisqu'Horace
> est Romain
> J'en ai reçu le titre en recevant sa
> main;
> Mais ce noeud me tiendroit en esclave
> enchaînée
> S'il m'empêchoit de voir en quels lieux
> je suis née.
> . . . .
> Je crains notre victoire autant que
> notre perte.
> . . . .
> Mes trois frères dans l'une, et mon
> mari dans l'autre,
> . . . .
> Je sais que ton Etat, encore en sa
> naissance,
> Ne sauroit, sans la guerre, affermir sa
> puissance;
> (Acte I, Scène i, 25-28; 32; 36;
> 39-40)

She is torn between her Alban roots and her Roman
nationality. In the event of a war between Alba and
Rome, Sabine has much to lose. She will either suffer
the loss of her three brothers or that of her husband
if war breaks out. Although Sabine is now Roman by
marriage, she has not relinquished her patriotism for
Alba. If marriage were as harsh as slavery, only then
would she be forced to forget her country; however,
her marriage tie to Horace cannot obliterate her
feelings for Alba and her three brothers. Lancaster
considers Sabine a familiar type of female character
in the theater: ". . . Sabine, is typical of women
married to men of a country with which their own is at
war. Her situation is that of Queen Anne of Austria
herself."[142] It is interesting that Lancaster has
drawn this parallel because marriage uprooted both
Sabine and Anne of Austria and their situations were
similar: their homeland was engaged in war with their
adopted country, one which they were forced to adopt
through marriage.

Sabine continues to reveal her innermost
thoughts. It seems that she has strong, negative
feelings about being Roman: "Tant qu'un espoir de
paix a pu flatter ma peine, / Qui, j'ai fait vanité
d'être toute Romaine" (Acte I, Scène i, 71-72). She
also cannot suppress her continued patriotism towards
Alba, her homeland:

> Si j'ai vu Rome heureuse avec quelque
> regret,
> Soudain j'ai condamné ce mouvement
> secret:
> Et si j'ai ressenti, dans ses destins
> contraires,
> Quelque maligne joie en faveur de mes
> frères,
> Soudain, pour l'étouffer rappelant ma
> raison,
> J'ai pleuré quand la gloire entroit
> dans leur maison.
> (Acte I, Scène i, 73-78)

It is not possible for her to sacrifice her Alban ties
for the sake of her marriage and husband. She cannot
celebrate any Roman conquest that occurs at the
expense of Alba. Sabine feels much shame concerning
her grief over the impending war:

> J'ai honte de montrer tant de
> mélancolie,

> Et mon coeur, accablé de mille déplaisirs,
> Cherche la solitude à cacher ses soupirs.
>
> (Acte I, Scène i, 132-34)

Because of the grief Sabine feels, she must retreat to her house and avoid seeing Camille from whom she believes she must hide her ambivalence about being Roman. Sabine's dilemma is caused by the necessity to overcome private feelings of grief for the benefit of the public good. She is torn by the extreme difficulty of such an undertaking because she is being asked to ignore her natural feelings and her love for her native country.

Before Curiace's unexpected visit to her house, Camille revealed her private feelings on the war and its effects. She states that she will not accept any husband who has murdered other men in war (Acte I, Scène ii, 229-32). When Curiace enters, he assures Camille he has not yet shed any blood (Acte I, Scène iii, 235-40), and that she should not fear for his safety. Camille misunderstands his reassurances and believes that he prefers her love to the good of his country:

> Curiace, il suffit, je devine le reste:
> Tu fuis une bataille à tes voeux si funeste,
> Et ton coeur, tout à moi, pour ne me perdre pas,
> Dérobe à ton pays le secours de ton bras.
>
> (Acte I, Scène iii, 243-46)

Nadal finds Camille's assertion that she still loves Curiace, even if he is a deserter, admirable:

> La jeune fille a le courage d'aimer Curiace qu'elle croit déserteur. . . . Les choses du coeur ne dépendent plus pour elle de la renommée ou de l'estime. Tout ce qui prouve l'amour—au prix même de l'honneur—lui fait un devoir d'aimer davantage.[143]

Camille is courageous and individual in her thinking. She has taken great risks to inform Curiace of her undying love for him. Yet, this is a risk she was forced to take because of the unexpected nature of

66

Curiace's visit. She has exposed her most private feelings for Curiace and if they become public knowledge, she will be viewed as a traitor against her Roman origins because she loves a Roman enemy more than her country. Curiace's visit is shocking to her and she lives in fear of her father's authority if he should discover Curiace in her house (Acte I, Scène iii, 253-56). The result of this visit is that Camille reveals that, for her, love is a value which takes precedence over patriotism for a country that achieves its glory through war and the destruction of human life.

When the private feelings of the female characters in <u>Horace</u> become a threat to the political goals of the male characters, the public/private split is used to the male advantage. For example, when Camille and Sabine become too vocal about their opposition to a war between Rome and Alba, Horace arrives at an effective solution to silence them. Horace wishes to prevent any interruption of his duel with Curiace and his brothers by confining the women against their will:

> Mon père, retenez des femmes qui s'emportent,
> Et de grâce empêchez surtout qu'elles ne sortent.
> Leur amour importun viendroit avec éclat
> Par des cris et des pleurs troubler notre combat;
> (Acte II, Scène viii, 695-98)

The women will be forced to remain in their homes because their love ("Leur amour importun . . .") is an obstacle to male aggressivity. Horace wants to make sure that they do not get in his way with their grief.

Sabine informs Julie, her confidante, of the imprisonment forced on her and Camille:

> Vous faut-il étonner de ce que je l'ignore,
> Et ne savez-vous point que de cette maison
> Pour Camille et pour moi l'on fait une prison?
> Julie, on nous renferme, on a peur de nos larmes;
> Sans cela nous serions au milieu de

67

leurs armes,
(Acte III, scène ii, 772-76)

Sabine and Camille must await the outcome of the duel which no side will win in their opinion. Julie is the only link with the outside world that Sabine has. She informs Sabine of how and why the army separated before a battle began:

> Tel porte jusqu'aux cieux leur vertu sans égale,
> Et tel l'ose nommer sacrilége et brutale.
> Ces divers sentiments n'ont pourtant qu'une voix;
> Tous accusent leurs chefs, tous détestent leur choix;
> Et ne pouvant souffrir un combat si barbare,
> On s'écrie, on s'avance, enfin on les sépare.
> (Acte III, Scène ii, 787-92)

The inhumanity of a duel between two armies with such close family ties is recognized by the soldiers themselves. Sabine and Camille react to this news differently. Camille sees no reason for hope:

> Ce délai de nos maux rendra leurs coups plus rudes;
> Ce n'est qu'un plus long terme à nos inquiétudes;
> . . . .
> C'est de pleurer plus tard ceux qu'il faudra pleurer.
> (Acte III, Scène iii, 835-36; 838)

She simply believes that the interruption in the duel will only postpone the suffering she will inevitably have to face. Sabine, on the other hand, accepts the prospect of hope: "Sur ce qui fait pour nous prenons plus d'assurance, / Et souffrons les douceurs d'une juste espérance" (Acte III, Scène iii, 855-56). Camille and Sabine are in extremely difficult situations. Since they are confined to their homes, they can only speculate on the information they receive from the outside. The private domain can thus serve as a prison when male political activity does not wish to be hampered by the presence of women.

When Camille is ordered to relinquish her grief over Curiace's death, she learns that the public good must take precedence over domestic losses. Her father, Le Vieil Horace, emphasizes male values when he states that all personal losses should always be subordinate to the good of the Roman State:

> Tous nos maux à ce prix doivent nous être doux.
> En la mort d'un amant vous ne perdez qu'un homme
> Dont la perte est aisée à réparer dans Rome;
> Après cette victoire, il n'est point de Romain
> Qui ne soit glorieux de vous donner la main.
> (Acte IV, Scène iii, 1178-82)

In other words, the private domain is subordinate to the public domain. Le Vieil Horace attempts to convince his daughter that Rome will repair her losses, and that her grief over Curiace's death represents weakness and cowardice (Acte IV, Scène iii, 1191-94). He is extremely insensitive to her grief, which she had to suppress for so long, and which she had to keep private. It is Sabine who renounced Roman virtue for its inhumanity. She clearly states the degree of a public/private split that is demanded of her and all women in Roman society: "Prenons part en public aux victoires publiques; / Pleurons dans la maison nos malheurs domestiques" (Acte IV, Scène vii, 1371-72). The total division between these two domains is precisely described by Sabine. This is a reality that is doubly hard for the women characters to bear because they must hide their grief, which is natural under the circumstances, and they must sacrifice their values for the good of beliefs they oppose. Although Camille rejected the public/private split by expressing her grief and wrath against Horace, while Sabine opposed it throughout the play, they were both forced to accept it either through murder (Camille) or silence (Sabine).

Emilie, through her desire and intention to act in the public domain, rejects the public/private split, which is imposed on her as a female. In other words, in the patriarchal world she inhabits, in Cinna, she is forced to live her life in the private domain, with its preoccupation of the family and personal ties, in general. It is not at all surprising that Emilie is obsessed with the account of her father's death, and that her hate for Auguste is fierce, since, as a prisoner of the private domain, she has had many years of inactivity imposed upon her, and she had had much time to dwell on the violent end of her father's life.

Emilie, like Chimène and Camille before her, will reject the split between public and private domains, and will choose to assert her rights and defend them by acting in the public domain. In a patriarchal world, such as Auguste's, the public domain is the political arena of men, where men engage in activities that are of the utmost importance to the shape of the world, whereas the private domain, the less important one, is the female realm, where women maintain family roots and ties and sustain life on the personal level. The unique sign of a Cornelian heroine is that she rejects the public/private split, and chooses to affect the shape of her life through political activity, which is, any activity she attempts outside of the private domain.

The limitations imposed on Emilie in the public domain comprise two levels. The first is spatial, in that as a female she cannot occupy male space: space assigned to male and not female activity, while the second is physical, since Emilie is forbidden on the social and political level from using physical means in male space.

Although, in the beginning of the play, Emilie can be perceived as a woman confined to her home as she awaits news from her lover, she rejects this confinement to the private domain, and the split imposed upon her, by choosing to initiate and organize a conspiracy against Auguste:

> C'est une lâcheté que de remettre à d'autres
> Les intérêts publics qui s'attachent aux nôtres.
> Joignons à la douceur de venger nos parents,
> La gloire qu'on remporte à punir les tyrans,
> Et faisons publier par toute l'Italie:
> "La liberté de Rome est l'oeuvre d'Emilie. . . ."[144]
>
> (Acte I, Scène ii, 105-10)

Implicit in her assertion to Cinna that she will be responsible for the liberation of Rome (110), is the fact that she will leave her mark on Roman history through her political acts. Emilie seeks vengeance for her father's death through a conspiracy that she has engineered:

> L'action s'ouvre sur la vengeance d'Emilie qui provoque la conjuration. . . . Par suite, Emilie conçoit la vengeance contre le meurtrier de son père comme un devoir familial et politique.[145]

Auguste's death will be Emilie's glorious act in the public domain.

Emilie will not only act through her political activity, but she also sees her cause (revenge for her father's death) as inseparable from the public cause (the desire to liberate Rome from tyranical rule). In this way, she joins the private to the public and destroys this split in her life. The conspiracy against Auguste unites her interest to the interests of all Romans. Examples of this can be found in lines such as:

> La liberté de Rome est l'oeuvre d'Emilie.
> (Acte I, Scène ii, 110)
> L'intérêt d'Emilie et celui des Romains.
> (Acte I, Scène iii, 156)
> Trahir vos intérêts et la cause publique!
> (Acte I, Scène iv, 306)

where Emilie's desire for vengeance is inseparable from the desires of all Romans for freedom from tyranny.

Despite the fact that Emilie rejects the public/private split, and ingeniously joins one to the other, the reality of this split can work against her in ways that she cannot prevent. For example, since Emilie is restricted from Auguste's space, and is only led there after admitting her guilt, she receives all of the news of the conspiracy secondhand from Cinna. In the same manner as Chimène and Camille, she must anxiously await news from the outside.

71

The public/private split can frequently act
against Emilie. However, she is unable to prevent
this. Although she instigated the conspiracy, she is
still not acting on her own behalf. She must act
through Cinna; therefore, she must inspire his loyalty
to her cause by urging him to be strong when he faces
Auguste (Acte I, Scène iv, 329-335). If Cinna waivers
when he is influenced by Auguste's munificence, Emilie
must set an example for him by remaining firm in her
desire to pursue vengeance (Acte III, Scène iv).
However, when the thought of this act seems treasonous
to Cinna, after his desire to conspire has weakened,
he blames Emilie for this act and reminds her that she
must depend on him: "Sans moi, vous n'auriez plus de
pouvoir sur sa vie" (Acte III, Scène iv, 962). We can
imagine what an irritant this reminder is for such an
energetic and powerful heroine. She is restricted
from acting for herself, and must always act through
another character, who may turn against her.

Two other repercussions of the public/private
split, which Emilie cannot prevent, are related to her
absence from the public domain. Emilie has no way of
knowing that Auguste and Cinna are exchanging her
behind her back: "Pour épouse, Cinna, je vous donne
Emilie" (Acte II, Scène i, 637). As Allentuch points
out, despite the odds against them, the heroines still
manage to determine the shape of their destiny:
"Objects of trade and vanity, for unlike men,
Corneille's heroines are abducted, possessed,
prostituted, exchanged, they contrive, nonetheless, to
master their destiny."[146] Emilie frequently asserts
that she is no one's property, to counteract what
Auguste might think.

Emilie is also cut off from news of the events of
the conspiracy. When Maxime appears in her house, he
claims that everything has been discovered and that
Auguste's men are about to arrest her. Maxime wants
Emilie to flee with him to safety by boat (Acte IV,
Scène v). Although Emilie has no way of knowing that
she is being tricked by Maxime, she refused to depart
and escape the consequences of her act. She also
discovers that Maxime is the one who betrayed Cinna.
Despite the lack of information she has, she is still
able to determine a course of action that is
consistent with her character. The public/private
split, which is a form of forced oppression, is
rejected and circumvented by Emilie.

Pauline exemplifies a heroine who consistently has to sacrifice her private needs to the public good. In <u>Polyeucte</u>, however, the validity of her sacrifices becomes questionable, because her father, Félix, fails to represent a stable political world. Under Félix's direction, the public good is everchanging. Pauline will make sacrifices in her private life whch will seem absurd in view of Félix's vacillating perceptions of the public good. Pauline will reject the public/private split which governs her life, in an attempt to avoid humiliation at the hands of Félix, and to determine a fate of her choosing.

Early in the play, Pauline complains of Polyeucte's indifference to her dream and her fears for his life. Pauline reveals her private thoughts or true feelings[147] concerning female influence on male lives:

> Tu vois, ma Stratonice, en quel siècle nous sommes:
> Voilà notre pouvoir sur les esprits des hommes;
> . . . .
> Tant qu'ils ne sont qu'amants, nous sommes souveraines,
> Et jusqu'à la conquête ils nous traitent de reines;
> Mais après l'hyménée ils sont rois à leur tour.
> (Acte I, Scène iii, 129-30; 133-35)

Pauline's complaints are justified since she and Polyeucte have been married for only two weeks. Her confidante, Stratonice, represents a view held usually by the older generation of male characters in Corneille, when she states that Pauline should not be alarmed by Polyeucte's secrets, because men should have privacy from their wives:

> Il est bon qu'un mari nous cache quelque chose,
> Qu'il soit quelquefois libre, et ne s'abaisse pas
> A nous rendre toujours compte de tous ses pas.
> (Acte I, Scène iii, 142-44)

In view of Pauline's deep concern for her husband's safety, so soon after a frightening dream,

Stratonice's insensitivity to Pauline's fears is an inappropriate response.

Pauline will begin to reveal her true story and, most importantly, her real feelings about her fate at Félix's hands. Pauline loved Sévère: "Il s'appeloit Sévère: excuse les soupirs / Qu'arrache encore un nom trop cher à mes desirs" (Acte I, Scène iii, 171-72); however, Sévère's rank was not high enough to please her father: "Je l'aimai, Stratonice: il le méritoit bien; / Mais que sert le mérite ou manque la fortune?" (Acte I, Scène iii, 184-85). Her father was the obstacle to her private happiness, and she was forced to leave Rome, her home:

> Mon père et mon devoir étoient inexorables.
> Enfin je quittai Rome et ce parfait amant,
> Pour suivre ici mon père en son gouvernement.
> (Acte I, Scène iii, 202-4)

She was also forced to make a political marriage to satisfy her father's political needs: "Je donnai par devoir à son affection / Tout ce que l'autre avoit par inclination" (Acte I, Scène iii, 215-16). In other words, Pauline overcame her love for Sévère in order to satisfy her familial duty towards Félix. Her marriage to Polyeucte was meant to solidify Rome's ties with Armenia. Despite her personal needs for love and happiness with Sévère, Pauline was forced to obey Félix and fulfill his political needs. In this way, Pauline's marriage is inextricably tied to the public good and Félix's ambition.

Pauline's dream also represents her true feelings about her situation. To the Romans, a dream was considered a mirror of a reality to come. Pauline views her dream as prophecy. She has dreamt that Sévère is still alive and that he has triumphed as a warrior; she has also dreamt that her father killed Polyeucte (Acte I, Scène iii, 221-44). Part of her dream becomes a reality when it is revealed that Sévère is in fact alive (Acte I, Scène iv, 269). Félix fears Pauline's dream only insofar as it affects his political strategies and personal well-being. Félix makes his demands known, and Pauline must see Sévère.

74

During Pauline's meeting with Sévère, she will unwillingly have to discuss the reasons for her marriage to Polyeucte. She will be forced to make public her private feeings concerning her fate at Félix's hands. She has indeed overcome her love for Sévère:

> . . . l'entrevue sera pour elle sans danger. C'est sans aucun doute, parce qu'elle a une grande puissance de volonté, c'est aussi parce qu'elle n'aime plus Sévère.
> Si elle l'aimait encore, elle n'aurait pu si bien se dominer au début de son entretien avec son père.[148]

But we must realize that her triumph over these feelings is very recent, and that she would prefer not to see Sévère so soon:

> Un grand trouble, dont elle a un peu honte, s'empare d'elle. Elle voudrait éviter Sévère, avoir au moins le temps de se remettre. Et Félix la conjure de parler, dès son arrivée, au tout puissant visiteur.[149]

We must also not underestimate the power of Pauline's dream on her feelings. Now that Sévère is alive, Pauline's fears for Polyeucte's life are much more real.

Despite the forced nature of this meeting, Pauline is in control. She will reveal her feelings to Sévère: "Pauline a l'âme noble, et parle à coeur ouvert" (Acte II, Scène ii, 463), yet, she is very lucid, and is aware of the reasons for her present situation:

> Mais puisque mon devoir m'imposait d'autres lois,
> . . . .
> J'en aurois soupiré, mais j'aurois obéi,
> Et sur mes passions ma raison souveraine
> Eût blâmé mes soupirs et dissipé ma haine.
>   (Acte II, Scène ii, 471; 476-78)

These lines indicate that Pauline has mastered or overcome her feelings for Sévère, and that this forced meeting cannot upset her control over her feelings. Although Félix decides her fate, she is still able to be self-determining. Nevertheless, Pauline stresses the delicacy of this outward control of her emotions:

> Ma raison, il est vrai, dompte mes sentiments;
> Mais quelque autorité que sur eux elle ait prise,
> Elle n'y règne pas, elle les tyrannise;
> Et quoique le dehors soit sans émotion,
> Le dedans n'est que trouble et que sédition.
>
> (Acte II, Scène ii, 500-4)

The last two lines quoted indicate the very nature of the effects of this public/private split on Pauline. Only through a constant expenditure of moral energy can Pauline, like other Cornelian heroines, control or overcome her real or private desires for the sake of the public demands made on her. It is not a divided Pauline who meets Sévère, but one who has already triumphed over her former feelings.[150]

Pauline arrives at a solution that will put an end to any future tests of her control of her feelings for Sévère. Pauline urges Sévère not to see her anymore:

> Mais si vous estimez ce vertueux devoir,
> Conservez-m'en la gloire, et cessez de me voir.
> . . . .
> Enfin épargnez-moi ces tristes entretiens,
> Qui ne font qu'irriter vos tourments et les miens.
>
> (Acte II, Scène ii, 539-40; 543-44)

These meetings will only torment them about the past.[151] Pauline proved that this meeting was without risk for her; however, she wants to protect herself from undergoing any future tests of will:

> Pauline franchit l'épreuve décisive: elle revoit Sévère. Ce n'est pas sans trouble, mais ce trouble elle le

76

surmonte. Désormais elle rencontrera
Sévère sans émotion. Elle lui demande
prudemment de ne plus revenir, et elle
a raison sans doute, car il ne faut
jamais jouer avec le feu. . . .[152]

She is also conscious of her glory, which she wishes
to preserve: "Je veux guérir des miens: ils
souilleroient ma gloire" (Acte II, Scène ii, 550), and
she wishes to return to the privacy of her home: "Et
seule dans ma chambre en fermant mes regrets" (Acte
II, Scène ii, 563), where she can rest and rid herself
of the pain of seeing Sévère. Pauline desires to be
alone in a place where she can rest from all the
sources of her inner turmoil: Félix, Sévère, and
Polyeucte.

Pauline insists on being left alone. She tells
Stratonice that she needs a rest: "Souffre un peu de
relâche à mes esprits troublés" (Acte II, Scène iii,
579), and she insists to Félix that she will not go to
the temple in order to avoid seeing Sévère: "Sévère
craint ma vue, elle irrite sa flamme: / Je lui
tiendrai parole, et ne veux plus le voir" (Acte II,
Scène v, 630-31). She will finally be able to rest
from all the difficulties she has had to confront thus
far.

Pauline's long monologue (Acte III, Scène i)
marks an important revelation of Pauline's private or
true feelings. She is very upset by Sévère's return;
she fears him even though she believes that she knows
Polyeucte and Sévère very well (Acte III, Scène i,
753-54). Her love is centered on Polyeucte, as is
evident when she defends him to Stratonice, and
justifies his dignity (Acte III, Scène ii, 788),
because he is her husband. Pauline has joined the
public to the private in her life. She was forced to
marry Polyeucte for the public good despite her love
for Sévère; however, she overcame that love and now
truly loves Polyeucte, thus joining her private
feelings to the public good. In this way, she has
rejected and overcome the public/private split.

The Qualities of the Heroine

In this section, the qualities that present the
heroine as a strong image of woman will be considered
and elucidated. It should be noted that although
Cornelian heroines share some strong qualities, the
manifestations of their strength vary from one heroine

to the next. The qualities that will be examined here have either been mentioned in a cursory fashion in previous criticism, or not mentioned at all.[153] Corneille's strong characterizations of heroines such as Chimène, Camille, Emilie, and Pauline, can also be easily linked to the feminist thought and writings, which were part of a tradition in his time.[154] Not only was the theater becoming more moral during the 1630's and 1640's, but more women attended the theater, a fact that undoubtedly influenced and supported Corneille's strong images of woman on the stage.

As Maurice Descotes stresses, Chimène's role must be treated as a major one: "Pour commencer, on se contentera d'observer que le rôle de Chimène est indiscutablement très long (plus de 430 vers, presque le quart de la tragédie), plus étendu que ceux de Rodrigue et de don Diègue."[155] This fact indicates and suggests that it must be analyzed on its own terms and not treated as an adjunct to Rodrigue's role. With this in mind, we will now consider Chimène's qualities.

A quality of Chimène's that strikes us at the beginning of the play is her intuition and intuitive powers. Although her confidante, Elvire, assures her that everything will work out in her favor, and that her father has chosen Rodrigue for her husband, Chimène senses that a complete turn in events will occur (Acte I, Scène i, 53-56). Chimène verbalizes this feeling of foreboding in the best way that is possible to her. Her intuition that something disastrous will occur is strong and she cannot ignore this feeling. She depicts a Heraclitean vision of a world in flux where human happiness is a difficult accomplishment. Chimène's intuition is a quality which helps Corneille prepare the tragedy ahead. After the dispute between Le Comte and Don Diègue, Chimène senses that something irreparable has happened, and through the use of the image of a shipwreck (Acte II, Scène iii, 448-51), she knows that she should abandon all hopes for happiness. Chimène's intuition serves her well, and helps prepare her for the moral struggle that awaits her.

Chimène's decisiveness and will to act are demonstrated by the fact that she will seek vengeance against Rodrigue. Her declaration: "Son sang sur la poussière écrivoit mon devoir" (Acte II, Scène viii, 676), is a daring one. Chimène, like other Cornelian heroines, is unique because she opts for action. She will defend her family's honor and her own through revenge. Charles Ayer emphasizes that there are two methods of revenge open to the heroines:

> Corneille employed two methods of revenge, by which the heroine might solve her problem in a way which should redound to her glory. According to the first method, the heroine declares that she will marry the man who will avenge her wrongs; according to the second, she undertakes the revenge herself without the intervention of a third person.[156]

The first method described above will be that of Chimène. Since physical action is not possible because of the "bienséances" in the theater and in the socio-political reality of a woman's role in the seventeenth century, Chimène will opt for action through the use of a third person. Maria Tastevin emphasizes the difficulty of Chimène's revenge and of her intention to act:

> La jeune fille persiste malgré tout dans ses projets de vengeance; la pensée de la mort de Rodrigue lui est presque intolérable, et pourtant, elle la demandera de nouveau, cette mort. . . . Elle veut faire plus pour son père que lui donner "d'impuissants larmes," elle est décidée à accomplir la tâche que son honneur et sa "gloire" lui imposent. . . .[157]

Nonetheless, Chimène remains firm in her decision to act throughout the play.

The moral strength of Chimène is most readily evident during her two forced encounters with Rodrigue (Acte III, Scène iv; Acte V, Scène i). She is engaged in a battle of virtue against the man she loves.[158] During her meetings with Rodrigue she undergoes a great deal of moral struggle:

> La jeune fille soutient une lutte intérieure, torturante et terrible. Elle déploie, pour parler contre son fiancé, une énergie intense.[159]

This is apparent before her first meeting with Rodrigue, when she explains the nature of her moral struggle to Elvire:

> Dedans mon ennemi je trouve mon amant;
> Et je sens qu'en dépit de toute ma colère,
> Rodrigue dans mon coeur combat encor mon père:
> . . . .
> Mais en ce dur combat de colère et de flamme,
> Il déchire mon coeur sans partager mon âme;
> Et quoi que mon amour ait sur moi de pouvoir,
> Je ne consulte point pour suivre mon devoir:
> Je cours sans balancer où mon honneur m'oblige.
> (Acte III, Scène iii, 812-14; 817-21)

The last three lines stress Chimène's moral strength in such a difficult battle. Her moral strength is constant and firm from the time of her father's death throughout the dénouement. Despite the intense demands of such a moral battle, Chimène never wavers in her conduct.

Chimène is a highly self-conscious heroine who has a sense of honor equivalent to that of Rodrigue. She is totally lucid about what she must do once her father is dead: "Je sais ce que je suis, et que mon père est mort" (Acte III, scène iii, 823), and she demonstrates her high sense of self-worth. The scene of her deliberation (Acte III, Scène iii), parallels that of Rodrigue's in the Stances, because her sense of honor is equivalent to his: "Je cours sans balancer où mon honneur m'oblige" (Acte III, Scène iii, 821). She is clear on her course of action and remains constant in her plans. The clearest indication that Chimène thinks in an equivalent manner about her honor, occurs during her first meeting with Rodrigue:

> Tu n'as fait le devoir que d'un homme de bien;
> Mais aussi, le faisant, tu m'as appris le mien.
> Ta funeste valeur m'instruit par ta

80

victoire;
Elle a vengé ton père et soutenu ta
gloire
Même soin me regarde, et j'ai, pour
m'affliger,
Ma gloire à soutenir, et mon père à
venger.
(Acte III, Scène iv, 911-916)

The demands of her honor are foremost in her mind.
Unlike Rodrigue, her battle to defend her honor lies
ahead.

Despite numerous tests of will, Chimène remains
firm and resolute in her intention to defend her honor
and pursue Rodrigue. Stegmann emphasizes Chimène's
resoluteness:

Chimène ressent tout le danger du
combat vertueux qu'elle mène contre
Rodrigue. Elle est déchirée, non
divisée et suit sans hésitation son
devoir de vengeance.[160]

Before Rodrigue's abrupt appearance before her eyes,
Chimène explains her course of action in a resolute
tone: "Pour conserver ma gloire et finir mon ennui, /
Le poursuivre, le perdre, et mourir après lui" (acte
III, Scène iii, 847-48). Chimène is firm in her
decision to seek vengeance for her father's death.
Even after Rodrigue's relentless pursuit of her (Acte
III, Scène iv), Chimène states that her original
intentions have not changed; "Malgré des feux si
beaux, qui troublent ma colère, / Je ferai mon
possible à bien venger mon père" (Acte III, Scène iv,
981-8). Chimène's resoluteness, despite the odds
against her, is one of her most admirable qualities.

Linked to her resoluteness is Chimène's
consistent nature. When Chimène learns that Rodrigue
has become a national hero through his exploits, she
declares that despite her love, which she has
overcome, she will continue to pursue him. Her
position has not changed and she remains consistent:

On aigrit ma douleur en l'élevant si
haut:
Je vois ce que je perds quand je vois
ce qu'il vaut.
Ah! cruels déplaisirs à l'esprit d'une
amante!

> Plus j'apprends son mérite, et plus mon
> feu s'augmente
> Cependant mon devoir est toujours le
> plus fort,
> Et malgré mon amour, va poursuivre sa
> mort.
>   (Acte IV, Scène ii, 1163-68)

When L'Infante warns her that her desire for vengeance opposes the public good, Chimène is again consistent in her determination to pursue Rodrigue:

> Ah! ce n'est pas à moi d'avoir tant de
> bonté;
> Le devoir qui m'aigrit n'a rien de
> limité.
> . . . .
> J'irai sous mes cyprès accabler ses
> lauriers.
>   (Acte IV, Scène ii, 1191-92; 1196)

She, like Rodrigue, does not see that there is a choice in affairs that concern her honor: "Après mon père mort, je n'ai point à choisir" (Acte IV, Scène ii, 1208).   Her consistency is a concomitant of her strong sense of honor and self-worth.

Chimène's resistant spirit is a unique mark of Cornelian heroines.   When the king makes a mockery of Chimène's determination to pursue Rodrigue, she asserts her rights and resists the king:

> De ma juste poursuite on fait si peu de
> cas
> Qu'on me croit obliger en ne m'écoutant
> pas!
>   Puisque vous refusez la justice à
> mes larmes,
> Sire, permettez-moi de recourir aux
> armes.
>   (Acte IV, Scène v, 1395-98)

The fact that the king belittles the seriousness of her pursuit of Rodrigue outrages her:

> La réponse du roi a été pour elle un
> véritable outrage.   Tant d'efforts,
> tant de luttes, tant de déchirements
> n'ont donc servi à rien! on ne prend
> même pas sa demande au sérieux!   Eh
> bien, elle prouvera qu'elle était

> sincère, et elle annonce qu'elle est
> prête à épouser celui qui tuera
> Rodrigue, elle appartiendra au vengeur
> de son père.[161]

Tastevin's interpretation is highly perceptive in her
description of Chimène's psychology. She understands
how Chimène was forced to offer herself as the reward
for the duel, in order to prove her seriousness to the
king.

During her meeting with L'Infante (Acte IV, Scène
ii), Chimène indicates her resistance. She is ready
to confront the king even if he refuses to grant the
justice she seeks: "Il peut me refuser, mais je ne
puis me taire" (Acte IV, Scène ii, 1205). The essence
of her resistance consists in her refusal to be
silenced. An example of this occurs after the king
has ridiculed Chimène (Acte IV, Scène v). Chimène
demands to be heard and resists the king's authority:
"De ma juste poursuite on fait si peu de cas / Qu'on
me croit obliger en ne m'écoutant pas!" (Acte IV,
Scène v, 1395-96). Chimène's resistance preserves her
from being victimized. She makes sure that her point
of view is heard and she resists any authority that
demands silence of her.

Camille's role has been a favorite among
actresses for centuries. Marty-Laveaux attests to
that fact: ". . . aussi Camille est-il le rôle de
prédilection de la plupart des débutantes."[162] He was
referring to young actresses since the seventeenth
century. Descotes compares Camille's role to that of
Hermione in Racine's theater: "Dans le répertoire
racinien, le rôle d'Hermione attire irrésistiblement
une débutante. Camille tient la même place
privilégiée dans le répertoire de Corneille."[163] And
finally, Tastevin mentions the range of Camille's role
and her popularity among actresses:

> Camille a été une favorite des
> actrices, ses imprécations donnant lieu
> à de beaux effets scéniques. Quant aux
> critiques, elle les a moins tentés, la
> "littérature" de Chimène ou de Pauline
> est beaucoup plus abondante que la
> sienne.[164]

83

She is, in fact, asking critics to give Camille more critical attention because of the importance of her role.

Horace is a unique tragedy in this study because it will be necessary to include Sabine and her qualities along with Camille's. Sabine's role is the longest in the entire play which prevents treating it in the same manner as L'Infante's role in Le Cid.[165] Ayer's demonstration that: "Corneille had a preference for two heroines,"[166] seems much more sensitive to Corneille's developing craft as a dramatist. Corneille, himself, proudly asserts that Sabine comes entirely from his imagination:

> Le personnage de Sabine est assez heureusement inventé, et trouve sa vraisemblance aisée dans le rapport à l'histoire, qui marque assez d'amitié et d'égalité entre les deux familles pour avoir pu faire cette double alliance.[167]

He created her role in order to make his play more symmetrical. This is implicit in L'Abbé d'Aubignac's speculation on Sabine's purpose in the play:

> Par exemple l'Auteur des Horaces a fort bien supposé le mariage de Sabine soeur des Curiaces, avec l'Aisné de leurs ennemis, pour introduire dans son Theatre toutes les passions d'une Femme avec celles de Camille qui n'estoit qu'Amante.[168]

Abraham is even more explicit on the utility and importance of Sabine's role:

> Although the seventeenth century admired this Cornelian creation, later critics have considered her superfluous. But she is of the utmost importance. First, there is the obvious matter of balance and structure. Thanks to her presence Horace finds in Curiace a brother-in-law, another self, whom he can fight with the same joy that he demonstrated in marrying Sabine (500). Furthermore, Sabine is necessary to

offset   not   only   Camille's   proud
individualism   but   also   Curiace's
capitulation.[169]

Most importantly, it seems that Corneille's own
justification of Sabine's role in the Examen of Horace
would carry the most weight, because he invented her
role in order to make his play more balanced in
structure and content. The purpose of this proof in
favor of Sabine's role was necessary to justify the
examination of the qualities of two heroines in the
same play. This is not to say that Camille is not the
main female protagonist or that Sabine is usurping
Camille's importance, but rather that Sabine's
qualities are important in their own right.

One of the initial qualities demonstrated by
Sabine is her sense of self-justification. She
defends her sex and asserts the strength of women:

> Approuvez ma foiblesse et souffrez ma
> douleur;
> Elle n'est que trop juste en un si
> grand malheur:
> Si près de voir sur soi fondre de tels
> rages,
> L'ébranlement sied bien aux plus fermes
> courages;
> Et l'esprit le plus mâle et le moins
> abattu
> Ne sauroit sans désordre exercer sa
> vertu
> . . . .
> Ma constance du moins règne encor sur
> mes yeux:
> Quand on arrête là les déplaisirs d'une
> âme,
> Si l'on fait moins qu'un homme, on fait
> plus qu'une femme.
> Commander à ses pleurs en cette
> extrémité,
> C'est montrer, pour le sexe, assez de
> fermeté.

(ActeI, Scène, i, 1-6; 10-14)

The underlined portions (emphasis mine), stress
Sabine's ability to bolster herself and to justify her
course of action during a difficult time. Cloonan
affirms this quality in Sabine:

85

> In _Horace_ the women initially see
> themselves as weaklings; their
> inability to appreciate the male
> fascination with violence and _gloire_
> fills them with guilt. Yet at the same
> time, behind the expressions of
> weakness and guilt there is an inchoate
> sense of self-justification, a nagging
> suspicion that they are right.[170]

Although Cloonan does pinpoint Sabine's ability to
justify herself, he does not seem to realize the
possibility that she is asserting her firm sense that
she is right, and that it is stronger than a "nagging
suspicion."

Sabine's strength lies in this ability to justify
herself. When Le Vieil Horace gives the women news of
the duel between Horace and Sabine's brothers, Sabine
again justifies herself and her values:

> Nous pourrions aisément faire en votre
> présence
> De notre désespoir une fausse
> constance;
> Mais quand on peut sans honte être sans
> fermeté,
> L'affecter au dehors, c'est une
> lâcheté;
> L'usage d'un tel art nous le laissons
> aux hommes,
> Et ne voulons passer que pour ce que
> nous sommes.
> (Acte III, Scène v, 939-44)

She has an intuitive sense that she is right, and when
she feels grief she must express it:

> Voyez couler nos pleurs sans y mêler
> vos larmes;
> Enfin, pour toute grâce, en de tels
> déplaisirs,
> Gardez votre constance, et souffrez nos
> soupirs.
> (Acte III, Scène v, 948-50)

What is implied here is a forceful self-justification.
Sabine, in essence, is saying, we are women, therefore
we are different from men, because we cannot hide our
feelings or suppress our tears in a situation as
extreme as war.

Coupled with Camille's intuition that her
happiness with Curiace is doomed, is her belief in the
predictions of the oracle. Once war is declared
Camille knows that Curiace, who is not Roman, has
become her enemy. Her father will never let them
marry considering their circumstances: "Jamais le
vieil Horace ne laisserait sa fille épouser un ennemi;
elle ne peut qu'obéir, se taire et pleurer."[171] As a
last resort Camille visits the oracle to seek some
solace. Camille listens carefully to the oracle's
proclamation:

> "Albe et Rome demain prendront une
> autre face;
> Tes voeux sont exaucés, elles auront la
> paix,
> Et tu seras unie avec ton Curiace,
> Sans qu'aucun mauvais sort t'en separe
> jamais."
> (Acte I, Scène ii, 195-98)

Camille is overjoyed by this prediction. She believes
that she will be able to marry or be united with
Curiace despite the war: "Camille, sur la foi d'un
oracle, croit pouvoir épouser Curiace. . . ."[172] When
Voltaire and Sarcey misunderstand Camille's joy at the
oracle's prediction, Tastevin attempts to put the
importance of the oracle in perspective: "C'est
gravement méconnaître l'importance et le crédit des
oracles à l'époque de la Rome primitive."[173] Camille
has confidence in the oracle's clairvoyance and she
gives much credibility to it.

Camille equates her power with the ability to
love. She is self-conscious and aware of the power of
women in love. She affirms that she knows Curiace
well because of this power that emanates from her
love: "Non; je te connois mieux, tu veux que je te
prie / Et qu'ainsi mon pouvoir t'excuse à ta patrie"
(Acte II, Scène iv, 543-44). Camille trusts and has
confidence in her values. When Camille learns that
Curiace will continue to love her despite their
hopeless situation, she knows that she must also die
if he is killed in battle. She warns him of this
because he intends to fight:

> Il faut bien que je pleure:
> Mon insensible amant ordonne que je
> meure;
> Et quand l'hymen pour nous allume son
> flambeau,

Il l'éteint de sa main pour m'ouvrir le
tombeau.
Ce coeur impitoyable à ma perte
s'obstine,
Et dit qu'il m'aime encore alors qu'il
m'assassine.
(Acte II, Scène v, 572-76)

Part of her power is her ability to love, which is a
positive force in her ethic; yet, her lover's
indifference to her love will prove fatal to her.

Both Sabine and Camille demonstrate much courage
through their opposition to war. They are brave
enough to be vocal about their values which oppose the
male ethic of conquest through war. They are
pacifists who believe war is no justification for the
loss of their loved ones. Sabine attempts to prevent
this battle altogether, which she believes is totally
meaningless. In an effort to deter this battle and to
make Horace and Curiace understand the brutality of
their plans, Sabine begs them to kill her. At least
then, they would have a reason for fighting:

Enfin je vous veux faire ennemis
légitimes.
Du saint noeud qui vous joint je
suis le seul lien:
Quand je ne serai plus, vous ne vous
serez rien.
. . . .
Qu'un de vous deux me tue, et que
l'autre me venge:
Alors votre combat n'aura plus rien
d'étrange;
Et du moins l'un des deux sera juste
agresseur,
Ou pour venger sa femme, ou pour venger
sa soeur.
Mais quoi? vous souilleriez une gloire
si belle,
Si vous vous animiez par quelque autre
querelle:
(Acte II, Scène vi, 624-26)

Sabine sees no difference between being murdered in
cold blood by Curiace or Horace, or their duel on the
battlefield. No matter which way or where it takes
place, killing another person is a brutal attack
against humanity. Camille is also consistent in her
pacifism and her ability to verbalize her opposition

88

to war. She cannot celebrate Horace's victory because
he has killed Curiace, the person she cherished most
in the world:

> On demande ma joie en un jour si
> funeste;
> Il me faut applaudir aux exploits du
> vainqueur,
> Et baiser une main qui me perce le
> coeur.
> En un sujet de pleurs si grand, si
> légitime,
> Se plaindre est une honte, et soupirer
> un crime;
> Leur brutale vertu veut qu'on s'estime
> heureux,
> Et si l'on n'est barbare, on n'est
> point généreux.
> (Acte IV, Scène iv, 1232-38)

Camille claims her right to grieve and let Horace know
what irreparable damage he has done by killing
Curiace. Sabine and Camille never waver in their
pacifism and they courageously oppose war.

Although Sabine and Camille are forced not to
intrude on male affairs, they are action-oriented and
cannot remain impassive when their values are
violated. Sabine wishes to act against the impending
duel:

> Prenons parti, mon âme, en de telles
> disgrâces:
> Soyons femme d'Horace, ou soeur des
> Curiaces;
> Cessons de partager nos inutiles soins;
> Souhaitons quelque chose, et craignons
> un peu moins.
> Mais, las! quel part prendre en un sort
> si contraire?
> Quel ennemi choisir, d'un époux ou d'un
> frère?
> La nature ou l'amour parle pour chacun
> d'eux,
> Et la loi du devoir m'attache à tous
> les deux.
> (Acte III, Scène i, 711-18)

She wants to do whatever she can to act against the
intentions of the males in the play, because she,

unlike the men, cannot "evaluate issues apart from the human beings involved."[174]

There are numerous examples of Camille's action-oriented nature. Camille is a highly individualistic heroine who fights as fiercely as Horace does for his values. She is a rebel whose resistance to the male ethic is her form of action in the play. One of Camille's most effective acts is her curse against Horace and Rome:

> Rome, l'unique objet de mon ressentiment!
> Rome, à qui vient ton bras d'immoler mon amant!
> Rome qui t'a vu naître, et que ton coeur adore!
> Rome enfin que je hais parce qu'elle t'honore!
> . . . .
> Puissé-je de mes jeux y voir tomber ce foudre,
> Voir ses maisons en cendre et tes lauriers en poudre,
> Voir le dernier Romain à son dernier soupir,
> Moi seule en être cause, et mourir de plaisir!
> (Acte IV, Scène v, 1301-4; 1315-18)

This curse has a powerful effect on Horace: "Camille a maudit Rome: une malédiction ne consiste pas seulement en mots exprimant une opinion, elle jette un sort."[175] Camille finally has an opportunity to take action and release the anger she was forced to suppress. Despite the limitations imposed upon them, Sabine and Camille take action against the men and their inhuman values, and manage to defend their own values through effective acts.

Emilie, like Chimène and Camille before her, has a long list of negative epithets associated with her character. Emilie has been called a vain woman and a parricide by Voltaire, an avenging fury, a woman who is really a man, and even a witch.[176] As Descotes has stressed, Emilie's is a difficult role for even the most gifted of tragediennes. However, it can be shown that the difficulty of this role actually arises from the complexity of a strong image of woman. When Rachel interpreted Emilie, she was christened the "déesse de la Vengeance," because it was thought that she accurately understood Emilie's characterization.[177]

One of the most important of Emilie's qualities is that she is politically-minded.[178] Her bold assertion: "La liberté de Rome est l'oeuvre d'Emilie" (Acte I, Scène ii, 110), and her association of her cause and the cause of all Romans: "L'intérêt d'Emilie et celui des Romains" (Acte I, Scène iii, 156), are examples of Emilie's political goals. As Ayer has stressed, when referring to all twenty-four Cornelian tragic heroines, they "find their chief glory in politics."[179] Emilie is an excellent example of political-mindedness in a heroine, in that she instigated a conspiracy against Auguste because he murdered her father.[180] Emilie gains the support of a large group of Romans, who, like her, want to liberate Rome from Auguste's tyranny. Her aspirations are highly political since she is engineering a conspiracy, through her lover Cinna, that is meant to free Rome of Auguste forever.

Linked to her political plans and aspirations, is her desire to act and make decisions. Emilie is action-oriented: "Elle veut agir."[181] Emilie wants something to be done against her father's murderer. She believes that Auguste, who seized power through Machiavellian means, must be punished for his crimes, the one that affected her own family, and those that affected many other Romans. When Cinna wavers and is unsure of the necessity of the conspiracy, Emilie is not frustrated that she cannot act for herself; on the contrary, she threatens to kill Auguste with her own hand, if Cinna will not: "C'est elle qui agira, qui se vengera seule. . . . Elle mourra, sans doute, en frappant sa victime, mais qu'importe?"[182] Tastevin assumes that Emilie would die, but her threat is serious, and the possibility that she could kill Auguste without dying should also be considered. Emilie is decisive in her choice to act. Not only is it her decision to begin the conspiracy and take action, but she never changes her mind. Unlike Cinna, Emilie does not waver, once she has made a decision. This is evident in her decision to pursue the conspiracy to its natural conclusion, which is Auguste's death. Although the conspiracy was discovered as a result of Maxime's betrayal, Emilie had the pleasure of telling Auguste, to his face, that she wanted him dead.

Emilie's independence is another one of her strong characteristics. She asserts her independence from Auguste: "Mais le coeur d'Emilie est hors de son pouvoir" (Acte III, Scène iv, 943). No one owns her despite what some may think. Auguste has been her oppressor since her childhood, and not the generous adoptive father he may think he is. We can see this through Emilie's rejection of his munificence, and through her desire to kill him. Emilie also asserts her independence from Cinna when he is unsure of her demands: "Sans emprunter ta main pour servir ma colère, / Je saurai bien venger mon pays et mon père" (Acte III, Scène iv, 1017-18).

Another aspect of her independence is her refusal to compromise when she feels her beliefs are justified. Emilie cannot think about her father's death in abstract terms. He was murdered in cold blood, and she, like Chimène, wants to avenge his death and her family's name.[183] Emilie has stated her terms to Cinna: he must kill Auguste if he wants to be worthy of her love. If he fails, she wishes this fate upon him: "Qu'il cesse de m'aimer, ou suive son devoir" (Acte III, Scène v, 1068). Emilie will not compromise; she remains firm in her desire for justice. She is a strong and determined individualist.

Critics frequently comment on Emilie's anger; however, they view it as a negative or unfeminine quality. Guez de Balzac thought Emilie was an "adorable furie,"[184] while other critics have felt that her anger was far from charming.[185] It is time to rid Emilie of the epithet, fury, because it connotes a negative view of woman, and it obscures the reasons behind Emilie's just anger. Emilie's anger is the result of a violent provocation. Her anger is not unwarranted. From her opening monologue, we can see that Emilie's anger has been growing throughout her childhood, and that the image of her father's death, which she never witnessed, had haunted her for many years (Acte I, Scène i, 9-16). Her anger is the most essential quality of her strength. It is responsible for the entire conspiracy, and now that she is no longer a child, she can answer to Auguste's provocation.

Another important strong quality of Emilie's character is her inclination towards resistance. Her resistant spirit is related to her refusal to compromise. Emilie resists Cinna's pleas for her to

terminate the conspiracy (Acte III, Scène iv), and she
resists Auguste's munificence to the end of the play.
In what is a meeting of the two central characters in
the play (Acte V, Scène ii), Emilie accepts Auguste's
conversion, which has been brought about by Livie's
suggestion to try clemency on the conspirators (Acte
IV, Scène iii, 1210), as his attempt to avoid further
bloodshed, and to be a just ruler. Emilie resisted
his favors throughout the play, because, until his
conversion, they were impure acts.

     Emilie's self-awareness is also a sign of her
strength. She has a clear sense of who she is because
of her high birth. She cannot live with the shame of
being "la fille d'un proscrit." She is aware of her
family name and noble descendance:

> Mais si fumante encor d'un généreux
> courroux,
> Par un trépas si noble et si digne de
> vous,
> Qu'il vous fera sur l'heure aisément
> reconnoître
> Le sang des grands héros dont vous
> m'avez fait naître.
> (Acte IV, Scne iv, 1311-14)

In an unprecedented declaration, she identifies
herself with all the heroes in her lineage. This
assertion also supports the theory of inversion in
Corneille's tragedies, and specifically in Cinna which
actually marks the beginning of the inversion theme in
Corneille's tragedies.[186] Inversion, or reversal as
MacLean calls it,[187] is the practice of endowing
females with male qualities, and males with female
qualities. This theme will be more fully developed in
Pauline's characterization. If we return to Emilie's
self-awareness, we find another explicit example of it
when she refuses to escape with Maxime: "Me
connois-tu, Maxime, et sais-tu qui je suis?" (Acte IV,
Scène v, 1331).

     The last quality that will be mentioned here is
Emilie's satisfaction with herself. This sense of
satisfaction is a result of her high self-esteem, and
her belief that she did everything to avenge her
father that was in her power:

> O liberté de Rome! ô mânes de mon
> père!
> J'ai fait de mon côté tout ce que j'ai

pu faire:
Contre votre tyran j'ai ligué ses amis,
Et plus osé pour vous qu'il ne m'étoit
permis.

(Acte IV, Scène iv, 1305-8)

When Emilie says these lines, she is in a state of turmoil. Maxime has just entered her house bringing the news of the discovery of the conspiracy. Her satisfaction with herself comes at a moment of lucidity, when she is preparing for her death, now that the conspiracy has been discovered, and she looks back on all that she has done up to this point (Acte IV, Scène v). At the end of the play, when Emilie and Auguste meet for the first and only time, Emilie is satisfied that she has told Auguste the truth of her involvement in the conspiracy and ready to accept the consequences of her act (Acte V, Scène ii, 1581-86). She is satisfied that she was able to express her justified anger ("un juste courroux"),[188] against a tyrant who caused her suffering.

The qualities that have been discussed here are manifestations of Emilie's strength, and reasons for thinking of her as a strong image of woman. In order to answer the question, "Is Emilie too virile?", it is necessary to understand what virility could mean when applied to a heroine. Examples and expressions of strength in women were part of a tradition in Corneille's time. They were present in the writings of moralists and dramatists. Corneille was depicting images of strong women that were part of that tradition from the 1630's well into the 1650's. It is well-documented that Corneille's heroines found great favor with the women in his public and with the "précieuses." Since, in any case, there is enough contradiction in criticism that addresses itself to the characterization of Cornelian heroines, it seems sensible not to confuse our perceptions of the heroines by referring to them using masculine terms such as virility. Tastevin addressed the accusation of Emilie's virility in the following way: "Virile, Emilie l'est donc, si l'on entend par là qu'elle a une énergie peu commune et qu'elle se mêle de politique."[189] One can also add that it is not necessary to obscure the image of Emilie by viewing her through masculine lenses. She is not a man, and should not be addressed in those terms. Corneille was not attempting to demonstrate how a female character could display "male" qualities; rather he was

94

depicting in tragic heroines, female strength and strong images of woman.

The importance of Pauline's role is frequently affirmed from a technical point of view. Descotes believes that Pauline's role is the richest of all Cornelian heroines: "Ce rôle est . . . écrasant (540 vers). Pauline est presque constamment en scène. . . . Rôle féminin sans doute le plus riche du répertoire cornélien."[190] More recently, Abraham emphasizes the importance of Pauline's dramatic range: ". . . Pauline has nearly one-third of the total lines in the play, and her role demands that the actress demonstrate a maximum range."[191] Despite Pauline's importance in the play from a dramatic and thematic point of view (we have already seen how Félix's entire political fate rested on Pauline's shoulders), Pauline's qualities fail to be examined in their own right, and tend to be measured in relation to the heroes' accomplishments or traits.

Early in the play Pauline delineates her moral strength. She speaks of her virtue when engaged in a moral struggle:

> Une femme d'honneur peut avouer sans honte
> Ces surprises des sens que la raison surmonte;
> Ce n'est qu'en ces assauts qu'éclate la vertu,
> Et l'on doute d'un coeur qui n'a point combattu.
> (Acte I, Scène iii, 165-68)

She is confident in her virtue, and arms herself for the ensuing struggle she is forced to endure with Sévère. When Félix affirms his knowledge of Pauline's virtue ("Ta vertu m'est connue," Acte I, Scène iv, 353), Pauline is also aware of her virtue, yet she dreads the difficulty of the struggle ahead, because of the extreme moral energy it demands:

> Elle vaincra sans doute;
> Ce n'est pas le succès que mon âme redoute:
> Je crains ce dur combat et ces troubles puissants
> Que fait déjà chez moi la révolte des sens;
> Mais puisqu'il faut combattre un ennemi

que j'aime,
Souffrez que je me puisse armer contre
moi-même.
                    (Acte I, Scène iv, 353-58)

If she had a choice, it is obvious that she would
rather not see Sévère altogether. Through her
struggle, however, Corneille is able to show how
Pauline is capable of great moral strength.

    When Sévère urges Pauline to show him that she
still loves him, she, unlike Sévère, wants to forget
the past and heal from the hurt she has endured.
Sévère bemoans the past, while Pauline wants to forget
it:

        Sévère: Je veux mourir des miens:
        aimez-en la mémoire.
                    (Acte II, Scène ii, 549)
        Pauline: Je veux guérir des miens:
        ils souilleroient ma gloire.
                    (Acte II, Scène ii, 550)

Pauline's moral strength is manifested in her ability
to overcome her feelings:

        While the heroic ethos disqualifies
        women from physical tests of courage,
        it challenges them, as well, to achieve
        inner discipline and some grounds for
        valuing themselves. They might set an
        example, as Doubrovsky demands, if they
        succeeded, where Corneille's heroes
        rarely do, in fully dominating their
        feelings.[192]

Pauline does set an example for Sévère. She is far
more concerned with her glory than he. Her moral
strength also makes her capable of returning to a
sound state.

    Although the political interest is less important
and less developed in Polyeucte, Pauline is still able
to display her decisiveness and desire to act. We
have already seen how, despite the constraints put on
her by Félix to obey, she actually chooses to act in a
way that is consistent with her character, and she is
able to make decisions. During her meeting with
Sévère, she shows her decisiveness when she insists
that they never see each other again: "Conservez-m'en
la gloire, et cessez de me voir" (Acte II, Scène ii,

540). While Sévère regrets his loss, Pauline decides that it is not good for them to see each other: "Enfin épargnez-moi ces tristes entretiens, / Qui ne font qu'irriter vos tourments et les miens" (Acte II, Scène ii, 543-44). She essentially leads the way in the decision not to see each other:[193] "Sauvez-vous d'une vue à tous les deux funeste. . . . / C'est le remède seul qui peut guérir nos maux" (Acte II, Scène ii, 546; 548). She also demonstrates her decisiveness when she refuses to go to the temple in order to avoid seeing Sévère: Sévère craint ma vue, elle irrite sa flamme: / Je lui tiendrai parole, et ne veux plus le voir" (Acte II, Scène v, 630-31). She intends to keep her word to Sévère by deciding to remain in her home.

Pauline's lucidity applies to herself and to others. She is fully aware that she needs a rest after her interview with Sévère: "J'assure mon repos, que troublent ses regards. / La vertu la plus ferme évite les hasards" (Acte II, Scène iv, 611-12). She knows that rest, which is actually comfort in solitude, will help her regain her energy. Pauline is also very clear about how she feels about Polyeucte after his conversion: "Je chéris sa personne, et je hais son erreur" (Acte III, Scène ii, 800). She affirms that she loves Polyeucte and desires his well-being, even though she disagrees with his actions. Pauline shows that she knows him well: "Vouloir son repentir, c'est ordonner qu'il meure" (Acte III, Scène iii, 906). She is certain that if Polyeucte converted to Christianity, he wanted to: "Polyeucte est chrétien, parce qu'il l'a voulu" (Acte III, Scène iii, 943).

Pauline demonstrates her independence in many instances. We have already seen how she maintains her independence from Félix by refusing to obey him, from Polyeucte by refusing to accept his desire to bestow her upon Sévère, and from Sévère by refusing to give into his demands that she give him signs of her love. Perhaps the most direct statement of her independence comes when she tells Stratonice that her sense of duty depends on no one but herself: "Apprends que mon devoir ne dépend point du sien: / Qu'il y manque, s'il veut; je dois faire le mien" (Acte III, Scène ii, 795-96). Pauline is also capable of depending on no one but herself: "Je ne prendrai conseil que de mon désespoir" (Acte III, Scène ii, 820). Pauline, like the other heroines we have studied, asserts her independence, which is one of her most essential qualities.

Pauline frequently asserts her rights to her father and to Polyeucte. Despite the constraints placed on her, Pauline is very assertive about what she feels are her rights. She speaks up to Félix and puts the blame for her predicament on his shoulders,

> Je l'ai de votre main: mon amour est sans crime;
> Il est de votre choix la glorieuse estime;/
> Et j'ai, pour l'accepter, éteint le plus beau feu
> Qui d'une âme bien née ait mérité l'aveu.
>   (Acte III, Scène iv, 965-68)

Félix is to blame for <u>his</u> choice of her husband and Pauline confronts him with that reality. The fact that she has a husband she did not choose, and a suitor she once loved who returns and makes demands on her, is all Félix's fault, and she does not let him forget it. Pauline is also very assertive with Polyeucte when she reproaches him for not loving her:

> Cruel, car il est temps que ma douleur éclate,
> Et qu'un juste reproche accable une âme ingrate,
> Est-ce là ce beau feu? sont-ce là tes serments?
> Témoignes-tu pour moi les moindres sentiments?
> . . . .
> Tu me quittes, ingrat, et le fais avec joie.
>   (Acte IV, Scène iii, 1235-38;
> 1247)

Pauline's anger is the consequence of Polyeucte's indifference, which hurts her, especially after all the sacrifices to her personal happiness that she was forced to make. She can no longer contain it: "Elle éclate en reproches contre cet ingrat qui oublie ses serments, qui ne se préoccupe ni de sa femme ni de la souffrance qu'il lui cause. . . ."[194] In this instance, Pauline asserted her right to protest and make sure that Polyeucte knew how she felt.

The clearest example of Pauline's resistance and ability to revolt comes at the dénouement. Pauline,

with all the anger she can muster, challenges Félix to
kill her the same way that he killed Polyeucte:

> Père barbare, achève, achève ton
> ouvrage:
> Cette seconde hostie est digne de ta
> rage;
> Joins ta fille à ton gendre; ose: que
> tardes-tu?
> (Acte V, Scène v, 1719-21)

Pauline will disobey Félix, once and for all, and she
does not hesitate to tell him so:

> On m'y verra braver tout ce que vous
> craignez,
> Ces foudres impuissants qu'en leurs
> mains vous peignez,
> Et saintement rebelle aux lois de la
> naissance,
> Une fois envers toi manquer
> d'obéissance.
> (Acte V, Scène v, 1737-40)

She even refers to herself as being "rebelle," and
again challenges Félix to kill her: "Affermis par ma
mort ta fortune et la mienne" (Acte V, Scène v, 1744).
Pauline has managed to break away from Félix's
authority, and she has revolted against his repeated
unreasonable demands. Her resistance to his authority
was always part of her response to him, and once
Polyeucte is dead, her resistance becomes revolt.

A quality which becomes increasingly more visible
among Corneille's heroines, and which is evident in
Pauline, is inversion. Inversion is also called
reversal, and it was a convention prevalent in the
literature of the 1630's through the 1650's in France.
One possible definition of inversion is:

> By such a scheme, men who act in a
> feeble, concupiscent fashion could be
> said to be effeminate, and women who
> act courageously, with decision and
> force of will, could be said to be
> masculine, producing a simple reversal
> of sexual attributes in individuals.
> It is clear that these polarities are
> used in this way by such writers as
> Hardy, Corneille, Du Bosc, Grenaille,
> and Le Moyne.[195]

Although the above definition does not apply well to Sévère's behavior, it does accurately describe Pauline's behavior. Pauline's characteristically Cornelian self-awareness demonstrates the fact that she seems to be more mindful of her glory than Sévère of his. She also values her glory more than Sévère: "Je veux guerir des miens [maux]: ils souilleroient ma gloire" (Acte II, Scène ii, 550). Pauline seems to pursue her glory with full knowledge of her purpose: "Mais plus l'effort est grand, plus la gloire en est grande" (Acte IV, Scène v, 1356). Doubrovsky sees female inversion as a humiliation for the male. Here is an example of how he sees Sévère's situation:

> Loin de se "vaincre" lui-même, comme il voulait et devait le faire, l'amant trop passionné est rappelé à l'ordre. Par un étrange et humiliant renversement, c'est ici la femme qui guide et élève l'homme, ce qui, du point de vue cornélien, est exactement le monde renversé.[196]

On an historical level, Doubrovsky's observation is highly inaccurate because he fails to inform himself of the fact that inversion was a literary convention, which gave diversity to characterization and helped vary character psychology. Inversion was a literary device, and it does not seem to have caused humiliation as a reaction, but rather pleasure among Corneille's female audience.[197] What is true of Sévère's inversion, which helps to establish Pauline's inversion more accurately, is Sévère's acknowledgement that Pauline is teaching him the way to generosity: "Et qu'une femme enfin dans la calamité / Me fasse des leçons de générosité" (Acte IV, Scène vi, 1377-78). And also that Sévère is measuring himself to Pauline: "Que Sévère l'égale, et qu'il est digne d'elle" (Acte IV, Scène vi, 1392). Sévère's reaction to this seems to be surprise and not humiliation. Doubrovsky identifies strong images of women as a source of male humiliation:

> Doubrovsky acknowledges that in Corneille's theater the "feminine" or "masculine" nature can be given to either sex. But then he characterizes the plays in which women take the lead as illustrating an "inversion des sexes,"--which is to insist, in a slightly different way from Lanson,

that the "masculine principle" is masculine property.[198]

What is pointed out by Allentuch is the male bias existing in Doubrovsky's criticism of female characters. Through the device of inversion, Corneille was able to create strong images of women, of which Pauline is an excellent example.

A final quality that has an important role in the play is Pauline's clairvoyance. Pauline, like Camille in Horace, has a dream which is prophetic. Pauline believes that her clairvoyance comes directly from the gods: "Au devant de la mort que les Dieux m'ont prédite" (Acte I, Scène iii, 126), which is supported by her Roman heritage: "Mais il passe dans Rome avec autorité / Pour fidèle miroir de la fatalité" (Acte I, Scène iii, 155-56). For her, her dream is a premonition of the disasters to come:

> Je l'ai vu cette nuit, ce malheureux Sévère,
> La vengeance à la main, l'oeil ardent de colère:
> . . . .
> Il sembloit triomphant, et tel que sur son char
> Victorieux dans Rome entre notre César.
> . . . .
> Ensuite des chrétiens une impie assemblée,
> Pour avancer l'effet de ce discours fatal,
> A jeté Polyeucte aux pieds de son rival.
> . . . .
> J'ai vu mon père même, un poignard à la main,
> Entrer le bras levé pour lui percer le sein.
> >   (Acte I, Scène iii, 221-22;
> >   227-28; 234-36; 239-40)

Those misfortunes would be the return of Sévère, who was thought dead, his triumph and wrath, and the murder of Polyeucte by Félix. Pauline's clairvoyance is not taken lightly by Félix, who fears her dream:

> Ma fille, que ton songe
> En d'étranges frayeurs ainsi que toi me plonge!

                    Que   j'en   crains   les   effets,   qui
                    semblent s'approcher!
                              (Acte I, Scène iv, 265-67)

especially since he has just found out that Sévère is
still alive.

     As the play progresses, Pauline's dream is still
vivid to her: "Polyeucte sanglant frappe toujours ma
vue" (Acte II, Scène iii, 585).   In fact, half of her
dream is already true: "La moitié de l'avis se trouve
déjà vraie: / J'ai cru Sévère mort, et je le vois ici"
(Acte II, Scène iv, 598-99).   Pauline's clairvoyance
is a leitmotif in the play. Her dream is a prophecy
of   the   future,   as   in   the   example   of   Sévère's
reappearance and then of Polyeucte's conversion: "O
de   mon   songe   affreux   trop   véritable   effet!   /
Voyez-vous qu'avec lui vous perdez votre fille?" (Acte
III,   Scène   iii,   928-29).   Her   clairvoyance   is   a
quality that lends much importance to her role.

78. In feminist literary criticism, the split between public and private domains in patriarchal literature and society, is considered a destructive force which we, as feminist critics, must address:

   We will recognize that much of literary appreciation is a personal subjective experience, and that to brush off such responses as irrelevant is only to perpetuate the destructive antinomies drawn in the Western cultural identity: between personal and public, emotional and intellectual, subjective and objective.

   Josephine Donovan, "Afterword: Critical Re-vision," in Feminist Literary Criticism, ed. Josephine Donovan (Lexington: University Press of Kentucky, 1975), p. 79.

79. Doubrovsky is a strong proponent of this male/female opposition, "Comme Horace, Polyeucte s'ouvre sur l'opposition de l'homme et de la femme. . . ." in his: Corneille et la dialectique du héros. (Paris: Gallimard, 1963), p. 229. See also, Charles Mauron, Des Métaphores Obsédantes au Mythe Personnel. (Paris: José Corti, 1964), p. 253.

80. Harriet R. Allentuch, "Reflections on Women in the Theater of Corneille," Kentucky Romance Quarterly, Vol. XXI, No. 1 (1974), p. 109.

81. "Femme forte" is a term which was used in the moralistic writings of France during the 1640's through the 1650's to describe women. It had its origin in the Bible. This term was characteristic of the new feminist approach toward the definition of woman, and of the greater prestige granted to women in France from 1630 onward. "Femme forte" refers to the conception of the heroic woman. For a complete discussion of the "femme forte" type, see Part III, "The New Feminism and the Femme Forte, 1630-1650" in Ian MacLean's, Woman Triumphant: Feminism in French Literature 1610-1652. (Oxford: Oxford University Press, 1977), pp. 64-87.

82. Milorad R. Margitič, "Corneille, Un Humaniste Intégral," Papers on French Seventeenth Century Literature, No. 8 (Winter, 1977-78), p. 153.

83. Claude Abraham, Pierre Corneille. (New York: Twayne, 1978), p. 57.

84. Margitič, p. 154.

85. Maria Tastevin, Les Héroïnes de Corneille. (Paris: Edouard Champion, 1924), pp. 4-5.

86. Tastevin, p. 5.

87. Tastevin, p. 6.

88. Tastevin, p. 13.

89. Milorad R. Margitič, "Corneille, Un Humaniste Intégral," PFSCL, p. 155.

90. Maria Tastevin, Les Héroïnes de Corneille, p. 18.

91. Tastevin, p. 21.

92. Of Corneille's silence from 1637 until the appearance of Horace in 1640, Antoine Adam (Histoire de la Littérature Française au XVIIe Siècle. Vol. I, Paris: Editions Mondiales, 1962, p. 519) indicates the following:

           C'est seulement au début de 1640, après un silence de trois ans, que le nom de Corneille reparut au théâtre. Avec un nouveau chef-d'oeuvre, Horace. Pendant ces trois ans, Corneille avait réfléchi sur l'art dramatique, étudié les théories récentes, observé la pratique des auteurs et les réactions du public. Entre le Cid et Horace, la distance est considérable. Elle révèle l'importance de ces méditations.

      More practical considerations can also be added to Adam's appraisal of Corneille's silence. In 1637, while creating the role of Rodrigue, Montdory, the actor directly responsible for Corneille's continued success at the Théâtre du Marais, had an attack and died. As a result of his death, Montdory's troop, at the Théâtre du Marais, was in a state of disorder, and Corneille found himself without the chief interpreter of his heroes. In addition to this inopportune death, Corneille suffered another great loss during his "silence," the death of his father, which involved him in much legal work. Corneille's marriage in 1640, also occurred during this silence. It is admirable that Corneille was able to accomplish as much as he did during a period of great upset and interruption.

It must also be recalled that since the "Querelle du Cid," which contributed to his silence, Corneille wished to win the approval of Richelieu by respecting the unities in Horace. Corneille's desire for the Cardinal's approval is obvious because the play is dedicated to him.

93. Maria Tastevin, Les Héroïnes de Corneille, pp. 47-8.

94. Charles Mauron, Des Métaphores Obsédantes au Mythe Personnel, p. 252.

95. Claude Abraham, Pierre Corneille, p. 63.

96. Serge Doubrovsky, Corneille et la dialectique du héros, p. 139.

97. William Cloonan, "Women in Horace," Romance Notes, Spring 1975, Vol. XVI, Number 3, p. 647.

98. Octave Nadal, Le Sentiment de l'amour dans l'oeuvre de Pierre Corneille, p. 180.

99. Eva Figes, Tragedy and Social Evolution. (London: John Calder, 1976), p. 113.

100. William Cloonan, "Women in Horace," Romance Notes, p. 649.

101. Octave Nadal, Le sentiment de l'amour dans l'oeuvre de Pierre Corneille, p. 181.

102. Ian MacLean, Woman Triumphant: Feminism in French Literature 1610-1652. (Oxford: Oxford University Press, 1977), p. 187.

103. William Cloonan, "Women in Horace," p. 648.

104. Ian MacLean, Woman Triumphant: Feminism in French Literature 1610-1652, p. 243.

105. William Cloonan, "Women in Horace," p. 650.

106. Maria Tastevin, Les Héroïnes de Corneille, p. 60.

107. Tastevin, p. 60.

108. Tastevin, pp. 66-67.

109. William Cloonan, "Women in Horace," p. 651.

110. Maria Tastevin, Les Héroïnes de Corneille (Paris: Edouard Champion, 1924), p. 70.

111. Jacques Maurens, La Tragédie sans tragique. Le néostoïcisme dans l'oeuvre de Pierre Corneille. (Paris: Armand Colin, 1966), p. 280.

112. André Stegmann, L'Héroisme Cornelien. (Paris: Armand Colin, 1968), Vol. II, p. 585.

113. It is curious that Serge Doubrovsky in Corneille et la dialectique du héros (Paris: Gallimard, 1963), p. 191, refers to Emilie's vengeance as Machiavellian and does not refer to Auguste's tyranny in the same terms. This seems inappropriate because Emilie has committed no act of violence.

114. Tastevin, pp. 78-79.

115. Corneille suggests Auguste's conversion in his Discours de la Tragédie, ed. Ch. Marty-Laveaux, Oeuvres de P. Corneille, Vol. I (Paris: Hachette, 1862), p. 69:
> Cinna et son Emilie ne pèchent point contre la règle en ne perdant point Auguste, puisque la conspiration découverte les en met dans l'impuissance, et qu'il faudroit qu'ils n'eussent aucune teinture d'humanité, si une clémence si peu attendue ne dissipoit toute leur haine.

The underlined words (emphasis mine) imply Auguste's conversion.

116. Maria Tastevin, Les Héroïnes de Corneille, p. 87.

117. Doubrovsky is a strong proponent of the idea of a male/female opposition in his: Corneille et la dialectique du héros. (Paris: Gallimard, 1963), p. 229. See also, Charles Mauron, Des Métaphores Obsédantes au Mythe Personnel. (Paris: José Corti, 1964), p. 253.

118. Maria Tastevin, <u>Les</u> <u>Héroïnes</u> <u>de</u> <u>Corneille</u>. (Paris: Edouard Champion, 1924), p. 103.

119. Charles C. Ayer, <u>The</u> <u>Tragic</u> <u>Heroines</u> <u>of</u> <u>Pierre</u> <u>Corneille</u>. (Strassburg: Heitz, 1898), p. 45.

120. Charles Mauron, <u>Des</u> <u>Métaphores</u> <u>Obsédantes</u> <u>au</u> <u>Mythe</u> <u>Personnel</u>. (Paris: José Corti, 1964), p. 262.

121. Both Allentuch and Descotes recount the story of the Dauphine at the court of Louis XIV who characterized Pauline as, "la plus honnête femme du monde qui n'aime point du tout son mari." See Harriet R. Allentuch, "Pauline and the Princesse de Clèves," <u>Modern</u> <u>Language</u> <u>Quarterly</u>, Vol. XXX, Number 2 (June, 1969), p. 171; Maurice Descotes, <u>Les</u> <u>Grands</u> <u>Rôles</u> <u>du</u> <u>Théâtre</u> <u>de</u> <u>Corneille</u>. (Paris: PUF, 1962), p. 208; p. 223.

122. Octave Nadal, <u>Le</u> <u>sentiment</u> <u>de</u> <u>l'amour</u> <u>dans</u> <u>l'oeuvre</u> <u>de</u> <u>Pierre</u> <u>Corneille</u>. (Paris: Gallimard, 1948), p. 202.

123. Harriet R. Allentuch, "Pauline and the Princesse de Clèves," <u>Modern</u> <u>Language</u> <u>Quarterly</u>, Vol. XXX, Number 2 (June, 1969), p. 176.

124. Maria Tastevin, <u>Les</u> <u>Héroïnes</u> <u>de</u> <u>Corneille</u>, p. 106.

125. Octave Nadal, <u>Le</u> <u>sentiment</u> <u>de</u> <u>l'amour</u> <u>dans</u> <u>l'oeuvre</u> <u>de</u> <u>Pierre</u> <u>Corneille</u>. (Paris: Gallimard, 1948), p. 204.

126. Tastevin, p. 13.

127. Allentuch, pp. 171-72.

128. Allentuch, p. 177.

129. Henry Carrington Lancaster, <u>A</u> <u>History</u> <u>of</u> <u>French</u> <u>Dramatic</u> <u>Literature</u> <u>in</u> <u>the</u> <u>Seventeenth</u> <u>Century</u>, Part II, Vol. I (Baltimore: Johns Hopkins, 1932), p. 325-26.

130. Harriet R. Allentuch, "Reflections on Women in the Theater of Corneille," <u>Kentucky</u> <u>Romance</u> <u>Quarterly</u>, Vol. XXI, Number 1 (1974), p. 106.

131. See lines 339-45; 346-49; 351-2 in Vol. III of Oeuvres de Pierre Corneille. Charles Marty-Laveaux, ed.

132. Allentuch, "Reflections on Women . . . ," p. 105.

133. Harriet R. Allentuch, "Pauline and the Princesse de Clèves," Modern Language Quarterly, pp. 178-79.

134. Allentuch, "Pauline and the Princesse de Clèves," p. 181.

135. Maria Tastevin, Les Héroïnes de Corneille, p. 126.

136. Pierre Corneille, Avertissement of Le Cid in Oeuvres de Pierre Corneille, Vol. III, ed. Charles Marty-Laveaux (Paris: Hachette, 1862), p. 83.

137. Octave Nadal, Le sentiment de l'amour dans l'oeuvre de Pierre Corneille (Paris: Gallimard, 1948), p. 171.

138. Charles Mauron, Des Métaphores Obsédantes au Mythe Personnel (Paris: Librairie José Corti, 1964), p.256.

139. Maria Tastevin, Les Héroïnes de Corneille, p. 10.

140. Tastevin, p. 11.

141. Nadal, p. 170.

142. Henry Carrington Lancaster, A History of French Dramatic Literature in the Seventeenth Century, Part II, The Period of Corneille, Vol. I (Baltimore: Johns Hopkins, 1932), p. 307.

143. Octave Nadal, Le sentiment de l'amour dans l'oeuvre de Pierre Corneille, p. 182.

144. Emilie is speaking to Cinna.

145. Marie-Odile Sweetser, La Dramaturgie de Corneille. (Genève-Paris: Droz, 1977), p. 119.

146. Harriet R. Allentuch, "Reflections on Women in the Theater of Corneille," Kentucky Romance Quarterly, 1974, Vol. XXI, Number 1, p. 109.

147. Allentuch, p. 179. Here Allentuch stresses that Pauline is in the privacy of her home where she is free to lament the powerlessness that women experience.

148. Tastevin, pp. 113-14.

149. Tastevin, p. 113.

150. See Octave Nadal, Le sentiment de l'amour dans l'oeuvre de Pierre Corneille, p. 202.

151. See Harriet R. Allentuch, "Pauline and the Princesse de Clèves," Modern Language Quarterly, p. 180.

152. Tastevin, p. 116.

153. See "Introduction" of this study.

154. See Ian MacLean, Woman Triumphant. Feminism in French Literature 1610-152 (Oxford: Oxford University Press, 1977), pp. 25-87. (Anyone of Corneille's tragic heroines could be linked to this tradition of writings on female heroic behavior.)

155. Maurice Descotes, Les Grands Rôles du Théâtre de Corneille (Paris: Presses Universitaires de France, 1962), p. 92.

156. Charles Ayer, The Tragic Heroines of Pierre Corneille (Strassburg: Heitz, 1898), pp. 48-9.

157. Maria Tastevin, Les Héroïnes de Corneille, p. 11.

158. See André Stegmann, L'Héroïsme Cornélien. Genèse et Signification, Vol. II (Paris: Armand Colin, 1968), p. 440.

159. Tastevin, p. 7.

160. Stegmann, p. 440.

161. Tastevin, p. 20.

162. Charles Marty-Laveaux, Oeuvres de Pierre Corneille, Vol. III, p. 253.

163. Maurice Descotes, Les Grands Rôles du Théâtre de Corneille, p. 143.

164. Maria Tastevin, _Les Héroïnes de Corneille_, pp. 63-4.

165. Descotes, p. 121.

166. Charles Ayer, _The Tragic Heroines of Pierre Corneille_ (Strassburg: Heitz, 1898), p. 27.

167. _Examen d'Horace_ (Oeuvres de Pierre Corneille, ed. Charles Marty-Laveaux, Vol. III), p. 277. (Voltaire and Lancaster are the chief opponents of Sabine's role.)

168. L'Abbé d'Aubignac, _La Pratique du Théâtre_, ed. Pierre Martino (1657; rpt. Paris: Librairie Ancienne Honoré Champion, 1927), p. 88.

169. Claude Abraham, _Pierre Corneille_, p. 64.

170. William Cloonan, "Women in _Horace_," _Romance Notes_, p. 647.

171. Maria Tastevin, _Les Héroïnes de Corneille_, p. 40.

172. Roger Lathuillère, _La Préciosité_. Vol. I (Genève: Droz, 1966), p. 491.

173. Tastevin, p. 43.

174. William Cloonan, "Women in _Horace_," p. 648.

175. Georges Couton, _Corneille_ (Paris: Hatier, 1969), p. 58.

176. Voltaire, _Commentaires sur Corneille_ (Paris: Firmin-Didot, 1800), pp. 130-131; 133; Charles Ayer, _The Tragic Heroines of Corneille_, p. 85; Roger Zuber, "La Conversion d'Emilie," _Héroïsme et Creation Littéraire Sous Les Règnes D'Henri IV et De Louis XIII_ (Paris: Klincksieck, 1974), p. 263; 268.

177. Maurice Descotes, _Les Grands Rôles du Théâtre de Corneille_ (Paris: PUF, 1962), pp. 179-94; 190.

178. This term is used by Henry Carrington Lancaster to refer to certain women of Corneille's time who were politically-minded. (_A History of French Dramatic Literature in the Seventeenth Century_, Part II, Vol. I, Baltimore: Johns Hopkins, 1932, p. 316.)

179. Charles Ayer, The Tragic Heroines of Pierre Corneille. (Strassburg: Heitz, 1898), p. 64.

180. See Marie-Odile Sweetser, La Dramaturgie de Corneille, p. 119; Maria Tastevin, Les Héroïnes de Corneille, p. 74.

181. Tastevin, p. 72.

182. Tastevin, p. 81.

183. Lancaster, p. 314. (Here, Lancaster compares Emilie to Chimène who is also seeking vengeance against her father's murderer.) Also, see Sweetser, p. 119.

184. Jean Louis Guez de Balzac, Lettre IX, A Monsieur Corneille, le 17 janvier 1643, in Lettres Choisies Du Sieur De Balzac (Leiden: Chez les Elseviers, 1652), p. 354.

185. Voltaire, Lanson, Doubrovsky, and most recently Zuber.

186. The inversion theme has usually been thought to begin in Rodogune (see Doubrovsky); however, one can trace it back to Cinna. (See also, Harriet Allentuch, "The Problem of Cinna," p. 881; p. 883; p. 885.

187. Ian MacLean, Woman Triumphant. Feminism in French Literature 1610-1652. (Oxford: Oxford University Press, 1977), pp. 166-167.

188. Emilie refers to her anger as being just, while she is in the presence of Auguste. See Act V, Scene ii, 1603.

189. Maria Tastevin, Les Héroïnes de Corneille, p. 100.

190. Maurice Descotes, Les Grands Rôles du Théâtre de Corneille. (Paris: PUF, 1962), p. 209.

191. Claude Abraham, Pierre Corneille. (New York: Twayne, 1978), p. 74.

192. Harriet R. Allentuch, "Reflections on Women in the Theater of Corneille," Kentucky Romance Quarterly, p. 103.

193. In Harriet R. Allentuch's article, "Pauline and the Princesse de Clèves," (Modern Language Quarterly, Vol. XXX, Number 2 (June 1969), p. 180), she stresses Pauline's role in this decision: "Aware of Sévère's suffering, she manages to convince him both of her love and of the necessity for accepting their continued separation."

194. Tastevin, p. 124.

195. Ian MacLean, Woman Triumphant, Feminism in French Literature 1610-1652. (Oxford: Oxford University Press, 1977), p. 250.

196. Serge Doubrovsky, Corneille et la dialectique du héros (Paris: Gallimard, 1963), p. 238.

197. The origins of inversion are traced to D'Urfé's L'Astrée in Ian MacLean's Woman Triumphant. Feminism in French Literature 1610-1612 (Oxford: Oxford University Press, 1977), pp. 156-171. MacLean also connects L'Astrée with the greater prestige given to women in seventeenth century literature through the 1650's.

198. Harriet R. Allentuch, "Reflections on Women in the Theater of Corneille," Kentucky Romance Quarterly, p. 99.

CHAPTER II

THE HEROINE'S EFFECT ON TRAGIC THEORY

Harriet Allentuch's finding that: ". . . Corneille writes more conventionally and simplistically as a critic than as a dramatist,"[199] is essential to an understanding of the importance of the love element in Corneille's tragedies. From a quantitative point of view, it will be shown that in his tragedies, Corneille will give the love element equal time with the political element. Are we to ignore Guez de Balzac's testimony on the favorable reaction of his contemporaries to Corneille's heroines,[200] or are we to believe that the love element is subordinate to the political element in Cornelian tragedy?

In his <u>Discours</u> <u>du</u> <u>Poème</u> <u>Dramatique</u>, Corneille displays his grasp of "Aristotelian" tragic theory concerning a suitable theme for tragedy:

> Sa dignité demande quelque grand intérêt d'Etat, ou quelque passion plus noble et plus mâle que l'amour, telles que sont l'ambition ou la vengeance, et veut donner à craindre des malheurs plus grands que la perte d'une maîtresse. Il est à propos d'y mêler l'amour, parce qu'il a toujours beaucoup d'agrément, et peut servir de fondement à ces intérêts, et à ces autres passions dont je parle; mais il faut qu'il se contente du second rang dans le poème, et leur laisse le premier.[201]

He argues in such a manner because he is responding to the scholars of his time, who attacked him for the unconventional types of heroines he created, and for the importance of love in his tragedies. Furthermore, it must be recalled that, in practice, Corneille presents a conspiracy or vengeance plot as inseparable from the love element, or to paraphrase Corneille's own words, as the foundation for the political element. It is important to note that there is an inherent contradiction in the previous citation, because Corneille states that love is the foundation for all the other interests and passions in tragedy, which would imply that it ranked first in the play.

Yet, Corneille concludes that love <u>must</u> rank second to the political element. The transition in Corneille's thought (". . . mais il faut qu'il se contente du second rang dans le poème. . . .") is not a smooth one. The fact that love in tragedy must be satisfied with second place implies that a higher authority dictates it as such, and that Corneille as a dramatist who held the pleasure of his audience as a primary goal realized that love in first place actually pleased his public most.

It is for this reason that much weight should be given to Allentuch's analysis of Corneille's conventionality in theoretical writing as opposed to his unconventional dramatic writing, in which he creates some of the most heroic and resistant heroines known to world theater. It seems unproductive and inaccurate to speak of the love element as being subordinate to the heroes in importance. It seems apparent that Corneille's restoration of strong female roles in the theater had a revolutionary effect on tragic <u>theater</u> in the seventeenth century, and not on tragic theory, where Corneille's response was more conventional.

The Importance of the Love Element

It is no accident that Corneille began <u>Le Cid</u> with his heroine appearing at once before the spectators, nor that he added the role of L'Infante. Both of these facts can be explained in relation to the love element and its growing importance in Corneille's theater. The same explanation can be offered for Rodrigue's two visits to Chimène's house.[202]

After considering the criticisms of the Académie, Corneille, in 1648, omitted the original first scene of the play between Le Comte and Elvire, and he chose to begin his play with a more powerful impact: he began the play with Chimène on stage. According to Jacques Scherer, the spectator's impatience to see the protagonist ("Impatience du spectateur") influenced the development of the dramatic technique that opened the play with at least one of the main characters: "L'habitude s'établit de présenter le protagoniste dès le début de la pièce."[203] An additional consequence of the spectators' thirst for the hero ("la soif du héros"), which included both heroes and heroines, was that of assuring the presence of the hero/heroine in all five acts: "la présence du héros dans tous les actes est assurée . . . dans Le Cid pour Chimène, Rodrigue et Don Diègue."[204] Of the three main characters just mentioned, Corneille chose his heroine, Chimène, as the first protagonist to appear on stage. In doing so he was probably catering to the tastes and growing influence of women on the theater. By eliminating the original first scene of the play, and by replacing it with the scene between Chimène and her confidante, Corneille speeded up the action of his play,[205] and also introduced the love element at the beginning.

In Acts I, II, IV and V, L'Infante's pattern is to appear on stage immediately after Chimène. She serves as Chimène's complement throughout the play. Couton perceives the importance of L'Infante's role:

> Elle apporte à la pièce une note fière et élégiaque; ses propos avec la gouvernante, avec Chimène, feront au drame des deux amants un subtil contrepoint. Sa présence s'explique encore d'une autre façon: il fallait, dit Scudéry, donner un rôle à la Beauchasteau. L'explication n'est pas non plus à rejeter.[206]

Couton, by recalling Scudéry's--in this case--accurate accusation, informs us of the practice in the theater of writing a role for a particular actress. In Corneille's case, this seems to be the most likely reason for the presence of L'Infante in Le Cid. Roles for actresses were in demand because they found great favor with the ladies in Corneille's audience. Descotes is even more precise and accurate in his justification of L'Infante's role:

> On est en droit de se demander si le personnage tellement contesté de L'Infante dans le Cid n'a pas été conçu uniquement pour fournir un rôle à une comédienne. Un des traits caractéristiques de la troupe de Montdory était l'importance des actrices, beaucoup plus grande qu'à l'Hotel de Bourgogne: la Beaupré, la Beauchâteau, la Villiers, la Le Noir--il fallait bien employer tous ces talents-là.[207]

115

by emphasizing the necessity to employ the dramatic talents of the actresses who were members of Montdory's troupe.

L'Infante's role should not be diminished in importance as it serves as a vehicle for introducing the love element in Le Cid.[208] The love element with all its power, so prevalent in Corneille's comedies, is introduced by L'Infante in this tragi-comedy. For Sweetser, L'Infante represents the generous rival ("la rivale généreuse"), while Stegmann believes that we should defend Corneille against himself, for considering L'Infante's role a detached episode in the play:[209]

> Aristote blâme fort les épisodes détachés, et dit que les mauvais poètes en font par ignorance, et les bons en faveur des comédiens pour leur donner de l'emploi. L'Infante du Cid est de ce nombre, et on la pourra condamner ou lui faire grâce par ce texte d'Aristote, suivant le rang qu'on voudra me donner parmi nos modernes.[210]

Although Corneille is responding to the criticisms of his chief adversary (Scudéry) when he admits that L'Infante's role falls into the category of a detached episode, he in no way considers her presence in his play as a failure on his part. In his usual fashion, he leaves Aristotle's Poetics open to at least two possible interpretations. Through his experience as a dramatist, he found that L'Infante's role was successful with his audience. Hers is also a role that lends much beauty to the play, and that integrates the love element in Le Cid.

L'Infante is the spokesperson for love and its power. She describes her love for Rodrigue in these terms:

> L'amour est un tyran qui n'épargne personne:
> Ce jeune cavalier, cet amant que je donne,
> Je l'aime.
>   (Acte I, Scène ii, 81-83)

Another example of L'Infante as the spokesperson for love and its effects occurs after she and Chimène learn of the duel that is probably taking place

between Rodrigue and Le Comte. L'Infante describes
love as an illness:

> Ah! qu'avec peu d'effet on entend la
> raison,
> Quand le coeur est atteint d'un si
> charmant poison!
> Et lorsque le malade aime sa maladie,
> Qu'il a peine à souffrir que l'on y
> remédie!
> (Acte II, Scène v, 523-26)

Her observations must have pleased Corneille's
audience, because they commented on the psychology of
love, a theme of great interest in the salons.

For Rodrigue's generation, the influence of
women, their salons and their values were much more
pronounced. When Rodrigue is asked to defend his
father's honor, his love for Chimène makes his
decision a difficult one. For the older generation,
love is merely a pleasure and not a value that carries
much weight: "Homme d'une autre génération, grand
soldat, mais non encore raffiné par la fréquentation
des ruelles, il n'a pas l'idée que les femmes peuvent
n'être pas interchangeables: 'Il est tant de
maîtresses!'"[211] Rodrigue, on the other hand, must
consider love and honor in his decision:[212] The
reality is that Rodrigue chooses honor over love, and
that he must face the consequences he did not
perceive: Chimène's defense of her own honor. It is
interesting to note that the love element and the
demands of the male ethic do not coexist well,
although Corneille is adept at blending these two
elements in his tragedies.

Rodrigue's visits to Chimène's house, actually
the reunion of the two lovers, were popular with
Corneille's public. At the sight of the two lovers,
the spectators reacted with much curiosity and renewed
interest in the fate of the lovers. Corneille
justifies these shocking visits because of the
beautiful sentiments exchanged by the lovers. In the
1660 Examen of Le Cid, Corneille describes the effect
of these two visits on his spectators:

> Les deux visites que Rodrigue fait
> à sa maîtresse ont quelque chose qui
> choque cette bienséance de la part de
> celle qui les souffre; la rigueur du
> devoir vouloit qu'elle refusât de lui

parler, et s'enfermât dans son cabinet,
au lieu de l'écouter; mais
permettez-moi de dire avec un des
premiers esprits de notre siècle, "que
leur conversation est remplie de si
beaux sentiments, que plusieurs n'ont
pas connu ce défaut, et que ceux qui
l'ont connu l'ont toléré." J'irai plus
outre, et dirai que tous presque ont
souhaité que ces entretiens se fissent;
et j'ai remarqué aux premières
représentations qu'alors que ce
malheureux amant se présentoit devant
elle, il s'élevoit un certain
frémissement dans l'assemblée qui
marquoit une curiosité merveilleuse et
un redoublement d'attention pour ce
qu'ils avoient à se dire dans un état
si pitoyable. . . . Je laisse au
jugement de mes auditeurs.[213]

When Corneille stresses that the reunion of the two
lovers had a magnificent effect on his audience, he
is, in effect, emphasizing the popularity of the love
element and the theme of distraught lovers. Through
his practice of the theater, Corneille helped love
become a legitimate theme for tragedy in the
seventeenth century. In this way, he prepared the way
for Racine's strong emphasis on love in his tragedies.

During Rodrigue's two forced entries into
Chimène's house, he forces her to admit that she still
loves him. Chimène's love is a theme throughout the
play; however, the demands of her honor had to be
chosen over her love. Rodrigue pursues Chimène
because he must be absolved for his actions by the
woman he loves: "Il est aussi un autre pouvoir, que
l'influence croissante de la préciosité élève à la
hauteur d'un absolu: c'est celui de la femme aimée
sur l'homme qui l'aime."[214] The evolution which has
occurred from the older generation to the younger one
is centered on the growing importance of women, love
as an ideology ("la préciosité") in its own right, and
the influence of women's values. Corneille
synthesizes these changes in the theater, i.e., in his
tragedies, by elevating the status of the love element
and by establishing a place for it in tragedy.

Before Camille appears on stage, Sabine
introduces the love element by giving a portrait of
Camille:

118

> Hier dans sa belle humeur elle
> entretint Valère;
> Pour ce rival, sans doute, elle quitte
> mon frère;
> Son esprit, ébranlé par les objets
> présents,
> Ne trouve point d'absent aimable après
> deux ans.
> Mais excusez l'ardeur d'une amour
> fraternelle;
> Le soin que j'ai de lui me fait
> craindre tout d'elle;
> (Acte I, scène i, 111-16)

She suspects that Camille loves Valère rather than her
brother, Curiace. Through Sabine, Corneille was able
to prepare the love element in his tragedy, and to
introduce the theme of rivalry in love. As Charles
Ayer affirms: "the necesary love episode, to which
his public had become accustomed,"[215] was a constant
in Corneille's tragedies.

In addition to love rivalry in his tragedy,
Corneille enhances the importance of the love element
by representing two types of heroines: the lover and
the wife. Corneille has his heroines justify their
positions as either a lover (Camille) or a wife
(Sabine). Sabine believes that as a wife she has more
to lose as a result of war, while Camille feels that
as a lover, there is no difference between what she
and Sabine will suffer. Camille's opening speech in
the play expresses this:

> Qu'elle a tort de vouloir que je vous
> entretienne!
> Croit-elle ma douleur moins vive que la
> sienne,
> Et que plus insensible à de si grands
> malheurs,
> A mes tristes discours je mêle moins de
> pleurs?
> De pareilles frayeurs mon âme est
> alarmée;
> Comme elle je perdrai dans l'une et
> l'autre armée:
> Je verrai mon amant, mon plus unique
> bien,
> Mourir pour son pays, ou détruire le
> mien,
> Et cet objet d'amour devenir, pour ma
> peine,

119

> Digne de mes soupirs, ou digne de ma
> haine.
>> (Acte I, Scène ii, 135-44)

Within the context of dramatic technique, Corneille found much favor with his public when his characters, male or female, were engaged in some form of love rivalry. Benichou believes that Corneille's public was fond of such scenes: "Nous en avons vu des exemples entre des héros masculins. De la même façon nous verrons les princesses entrer en lice. . . . Les scènes de ce genre entre deux héroïnes abondent: il faut croire que le public les aimait particulièrement."[216] Descotes reminds us that this technique still finds favor with the public during a nineteenth century performance of Horace, when two great actresses, Mlle Duchesnois and Mlle Georges interpreted the roles of Sabine and Camille, respectively: "Si, vers 1806, les représentations d'Horace sont si nombreuses c'est que le public est avide d'assister au déroulement de la compétition entre les deux actrices."[217] Corneille catered to the tastes of his public. The presence of the love element, in all its aspects, made a successful contribution to Corneille's tragedy.

Camille represents a more developed type of female character in French tragedy: the young lover. Herland stresses why Camille is a novelty for the French stage:

> J'ai dit que la tragédie de
> Camille n'apportait rien d'absolument
> neuf, j'avais tort: avec elle un
> personnage qu'on n'y avait jamais
> rencontré faisait son entrée dans la
> tragédie française: la jeune
> amoureuse.[218]

Corneille managed to make Camille's characterization more rich and complex by including more fully in his tragedy the psychology of love.

If we return to the love element in Horace, we find Julie, the confidante of both Sabine and Camille, questioning Camille on her meeting with Valère. Julie suspects that Camille loves Valère and not Curiace:

> Vous déguisez en vain une chose trop
> claire:
> Je vous vis encore hier entretenir

Valère;
Et l'accueil gracieux qu'il recevoit de
vous
Lui permet de nourrir un espoir assez
doux.
                    (Acte I, Scène ii, 159-62)

Camille explains that she had just returned from
visiting the oracle and that she was in a daze. That
was the reason why she was friendly towards Valère:

Je ne m'aperçus pas que je parlois à
lui;
. . . .
Tout ce que je voyois me sembloit
Curiace;
Tout ce qu'on me disoit me parloit de
ses feux;
Tout ce que je disois l'assuroit de mes
voeux.

            (Acte I, Scène ii, 206; 208-10)

The power of Camille's love for Curiace is obvious in
the above lines. Her belief that she will share her
love and passion with Curiace is unchanged. She is
most concerned with her love for Curiace and he is the
only man she loves.

     Early in the play (Acte I, Scène iii), the lovers
are reunited.   Camille is misled by Curiace's
unannounced presence in her house. She believes that
he has deserted the army and that he prefers his love
for her to his country (Acte I, Scène iii, 243-52).
Curiace thinks that his patriotism and love can
coexist (Acte I, Scène iii, 263-70). He best sums up
this belief by saying: "J'aime encor mon honneur en
adorant Camille" (264). He instills new hope in
Camille for the success of their love, and departs on
that note:

Et mes desirs ont eu des succès si
prospères,
Que l'auteur de vos jours m'a promis à
demain
Le bonheur sans pareil de vous donner
la main
Vous ne deviendrez pas rebelle à sa
puissance?
                    (Acte I, Scène iii, 336-39)

121

This meeting is a painful one for Camille because she is led to believe that there is still hope that she and Curiace be married.

The next meeting between the two lovers occurs fairly early in the following act (Acte II, Scène v). Because of the pressure of war, Corneille reunites Camille and Curiace in two successive acts, whereas in Le Cid, Chimène and Rodrigue met first in Act III and later in Act V. During the second meeting between Camille and Curiace, it is clear that Curiace has made his choice: "Je vous plains, je me plains; mais il y faut aller" (Acte II, Scène v, 542). Camille is shocked by his choice because he does not seem to understand its implications for her: "Quoi! tu ne veux pas voir qu'ainsi tu me trahis!" (Acte II, Scène v, 561). Curiace is definitive in his reply: "avant que d'être à vous, je suis à mon pays," (562). He will continue to love her without hope (570-71). Camille reacts to his indifference to her suffering with tears:

> Ce qui déconcerte l'héroïne, c'est le spectacle et le contact d'un monde où les hommes, et singulièrement le héros, subordonnent le bonheur amoureux à tant d'autres intérêts qui les flattent bien davantage.[219]

She is disturbed by Curiace's willed detachment from her and his choice of destructive values. Yet, Camille is resistant and she insists that she will love him even harder:

> Qu'au lieu de t'en haïr, je t'en aimerai mieux;
> Qui, je te chérirai, tout ingrat et perfide,
> . . . .
> Pourquoi suis-je Romaine, ou que n'es-tu Romain?
> Je te préparerois des lauriers de ma main;
>
> . . . .
> Il revient: quel malheur, si l'amour de sa femme
> Ne peut non plus sur lui que le mien sur ton âme!
>
> (Acte II, Scène v, 598-99; 601-2; 607-8)

she wonders if Sabine was luckier than she in trying to deter this battle. In any event, Camille knows that her love has been excluded from Curaice's choices and that she will suffer as a result.

Corneille achieves a crescendo effect by uniting both couples on stage (Acte II, Sène vi). This is the final goodby before the men go off to their battle. Sabine attempts to prevent this battle in a long speech filled with pleas and bitterness (613-62, but Le Vieil Horace arrives (Acte II, Scène vii), and the women and their grief are belittled by him. Le Vieil Horace, like Don Diègue, has little use for women: "The old Horace finding both Camille and Sabine in tears upbraids Horace and Curiace for allowing themselves to be affected by such feminine weakness."[220] He tells them to flee women's influence because they are weak and evil. Of this older generation represented by Le Vieil Horace, MacLean emphasizes that: "These figures associate women and love with 'oisiveté' and 'volupté'. . . . Their low assessment of women accounts in part for their sense of dishonour if defeated or outwitted by one of them. . . ."[221] Yet, for Corneille's public, the values of the older generation were eroding, and the strong influence of women and their values was being felt.

When Camille learns of her lover's death (Acte IV, Scène ii), she is forced to remain silent. Her father ordered her to be quiet before Valère's entrance: "Taisez-vous, et sachons ce que nous veut Valère" (Acte IV, Scène i, 1071). Camille must listen to the brutal account of Curiace's death without being able to react. Yet, the fact that he is dead for certain rids her of any attachments to this world: "Fini, le rêve de bonheur, Curiace est mort; plus rien n'existe et l'univers est vide."[222] All that she has left of her love is her grief, which she is forced to contain. When unleashed, her grief has turned to an anger that threatens the very foundations of the patriarchal world she inhabits. Corneille has made Camille's chief motivation that of human love. The love element figures strongly in a tragedy where male and female protagonists are severely polarized. Another dimension is given to it. Corneille gives the love element a serious place in his tragedy. He shows that it is not merely an embellishment of tragedy, but a theme that is fundamental to the preservation of human life.

Emilie, a pure creation of Corneille's imagination (like Sabine), was invented to add a love interest to the play.[223] The public of Corneille's time was far more interested in the love element, and the fate of the two lovers, than in the political element:

> The bulk of the testimony that has come down to us shows that Cinna's original public was far more impressed by the lovers than by Auguste and his clemency. The ending was considered happy because the young couple surmounted its problems, not because Auguste transcended his.[225]

Also, Couton states that the conspiracy is inseparable from the love element: "Puis, inséparable de la conspiration, une intrigue amoureuse."[225] And Voltaire stresses the influence of L'Astrée on the language of seventeenth century tragedy:

> En général, ces maximes et ce terme de véritable amant sont tirés des romans de ce temps-là, et surtout de L'Astrée, où l'on examine sérieusement ce qui constitue le véritable amant.[226]

He also emphasizes the great favor that the love element found with Corneille's female public: "Les femmes ne voulaient que de l'amour; bientôt on ne traita plus que l'amour. . . ."[227] Since Corneille's chief goal as a dramatist was the satisfaction of his public, the popularity of the love element in tragedy should not be underestimated.

Emilie opens the play shown in the role of a distraught lover. Her only hesitation concerning the conspiracy against Auguste is centered on Cinna:

> J'aime encor plus Cinna que je ne hais Auguste,
> Et je sens refroidir ce bouillant mouvement
> Quand il faut, pour le suivre, exposer mon amant.
> (Acte I, Scène i, 18-20)

Cinna is conspiring against Auguste because of his love for Emilie. Emilie realizes the risk involved, and the great loss Cinna's death would mean to her:

"Te perdre en me vengeant, ce n'est pas me venger"
(Acte I, Scène i, 36). However, Emilie's terms for
Cinna are clear and firm: if Cinna wants her, he must
kill Auguste: "S'il me veut posséder, Auguste doit
périr: / Sa tête est le seul prix dont il peut
m'acquérir" (Acte I, Scène ii, 55-6). The extent of
Emilie's love for Cinna does not seem doubtful,
especially after Fulvie says that the terms of
Emilie's love are too cruel: "Votre amour à ce prix
n'est qu'un présent funeste / Qui porte à votre amant
sa perte manifeste" (Acte I, Scène ii, 113-14).
Emilie is hurt by the pain of this possibility: "Ah!
tu sais me frapper par où je suis sensible" (Acte I,
Scène ii, 118). Therefore, it does not seem likely
that Emilie does not love Cinna, because the thought
of loving him is painful to her.

When Cinna speaks to Emilie of the other
conspirators, it is as a lover: "Tous s'y montrent
portés avec tant d'allégresse, / Qu'ils semblent,
comme moi, servir une maîtresse" (Acte I, Scène iii,
149-50). At the beginning of the play, Cinna seems
more interested in his status as a lover, than in
political ambition.[228] He considers the murder of
Auguste as a tribute to Emilie:

> Voilà, belle Emilie, à quel point nous
> en sommes.
> . . . .
> Mourant pour vous servir, tout me
> semblera doux.
> (Acte I, Scène iii, 249; 260)

Most of all, he thinks of it as a means of becoming
worthy of her love: "Quant à Cinna, le meurtre
d'Auguste est le seul acte qui puisse le rendre
'digne' d'Emilie, comme Rodrigue devait mériter
Chimène par la mort du Comte. . . ."[229] Lathuillère,
in his exhaustive study of "préciosité," also stresses
Rodrigue's perfect submission before his lover.[230]
Emilie also inspires Cinna to act by reminding him of
their love: "Souviens-toi du beau feu dont nous
sommes épris / Qu'aussi bien que la gloire Emilie est
ton prix" (Acte I, Scène iii, 275-76). Adam clarifies
the type of love they share: "un amour qui n'est
point lâche ni honteux, et qui se présente à lui avec
tous les prestiges de la plus pure vertu."[231] And he
also mentions Cinna's dependence on Emilie.

As lovers, Cinna and Emilie pledge their love to
each other, in life or death. First Cinna: "Heureux

pour vous servir de perdre ainsi la vie, / Malheureux de mourir sans vous avoir servie" (Acte I, Scène iv, 321-22), then Emilie: "Ne crains pas qu'après toi rien ici me retienne: / Ta mort emportera mon âme vers la tienne" (Acte I, Scène iv, 333-34). There are ample proofs of their love for each other, and that the love element is inseparable from the conspiracy. At this point in the play (Act I), it can be safely said that Emilie's love, and not political ambition, has the strongest pull on Cinna.

Corneille continues to introduce rivalry in the love element in Cinna through the character, Maxime. Sweetser reminds us that in Corneille's time rivalry in love was a characteristic of comedy, and that it took on an important role in Cinna: "La rivalité amoureuse, venue du schéma des comédies et très atténuée dans Le Cid et Horace, prend ici une nouvelle importance: elle va précipiter l'action au moyen de la trahison de Maxime."232 Since Maxime is Cinna's rival, he accuses Cinna of conspiring to kill Auguste solely to win Emilie in marriage, and not in the interest of Rome (Acte III, Scène i, 710-12; 717-18). After Maxime has betrayed Cinna and Emilie, he distorts the situation at court, and urges her to flee with him (Acte IV, Scène v). Maxime is asking Emilie to accept him as her lover (Acte IV, Scène v, 1346-47), but she rejects him in the same way that Chimène and Camille rejected their lovers' rivals. The additional love interest introduced through Maxime's rivalry demonstrates how Cornelian tragedy incorporates the love element in seventeenth century theater.

In the course of Cinna's deliberation (Acte III, Scène iii), it is obvious that he has been influenced by Auguste's munificence, and that his promise to avenge Emilie is wavering (Acte III, Scène iii, 875-85). His love for Emilie becomes what Doubrovsky pejoratively calls, "la servitude amoureuse."233 Cinna's dependence on Emilie as her lover seems to be constraining for him. What she asks is too difficult: "Mais voyez à quel prix vous me donnez votre âme" (Acte III, Scène iv, 929). However, despite his waverings, which are a grave disappointment for Emilie, she declares that she still loves him: "Je t'aime toutefois, quel que tu puisses être" (Acte III, Scène iv, 1033). She is surprised by Cinna's remorse and knows that other men would be willing to serve her: "Mille autres à l'envi recevroient cette loi, / S'ils pouvoient m'acquérir à même prix que toi" (Acte

126

III, Scène iv, 1035-36). She bravely asserts that she herself will kill Auguste. At this point, Cinna agrees to go ahead with their plans, but there is a strong tone of blame in his words (Acte III, Scène iv, 1049; 1057-61).

The love element, which runs throughout the play, is inseparable from the political elements of vengeance and conspiracy. Love diminishes and turns to blame because Emilie must act through Cinna, and not for herself. As noted above, in Corneille's time it is likely that the love element was much more popular than the political one. Corneille raised the status of the love element in his tragic theater and made a permanent place for it there, to the pleasure of his audience.

It is a well-known fact that Polyeucte was read by Corneille at the Hotel de Rambouillet, and that the approval of polite society could mean the success or failure of a play:

> The influence of polite society on the literature of the seventeenth century in France is not to be underestimated, and especially the influence of the ladies, those grandes dames, whose names add such lustre to the century of Louis XIV.[234]

Polyeucte was not received enthusiastically because of its religious subject matter:

> The Christian and self-renouncing overtones of the tragedy annoyed the Hotel de Rambouillet, Saint-Evremond, and other Cornelian admirers; Corneille maintained his reputation only because his audience so savored the impassioned whisperings of Pauline and her lover.[235]

However, the love interest between Pauline and Sévère was considered a redeeming factor of the play:

> Tous les témoignages concordent: c'est l'intrigue amoureuse entre Pauline et Sévère qui assura le succès de Polyeucte à la création, qui retint l'attention des spectateurs du XVIIe siècle.[236]

Much importance is given to the love element in Polyeucte, which found great favor with Corneille's audience. Antoine Adam stresses the emotional beauty and climate of this play:

> . . . il reste que Polyeucte est un extraordinaire chef-d'oeuvre de tendresse et de beauté morale. De tendresse d'abord . . . il est impossible de n'être pas frappé par l'émotion qui baigne toute l'oeuvre et qu'on ne retrouverait au même degré ni dans Horace ni dans Cinna, mais seulement dans les plus belles scènes du Cid.[237]

Several critics also lend a great deal of importance to the fact that Corneille had recently married,[238] and that this event in his life influenced the emotional atmosphere of the play. What is evident is that in "cet admirable poème d'amour,"[239] the love element is highly visible, and predominates over a weakened political plot. The influence of polite society had its impact on the success of Polyeucte, and on the place of love in tragedy.

At the beginning of the play, Polyeucte's opening speech attests to the extent of his love for Pauline, and his newly married state:

> Mais vous ne savez pas ce que c'est une femme:
> Vous ignorez quels droits elle a sur toute l'âme,
> Quand après un long temps qu'elle a su nous charmer,
> Les flambeaux de l'hymen viennent de s'allumer.
> (Acte I, Scène i, 9-12)

Polyeucte is moved by Pauline's concern and love for him, and as her husband, he is not indifferent to her: "Ces pleurs, que je regarde avec un oeil d'époux" (Acte I, Scène i, 43). Despite Néarque's urgings that he break all earthly ties: "Rompez ses premiers coups; laissez pleurer Pauline / Dieu ne veut point d'un coeur où le monde domine" (Acte I, Scène i, 65-6), he continues to be affected by Pauline's love: "Sur mes pareils, Néarque, un bel oeil est bien fort: / Tel craint de le fâcher qui ne craint pas la mort" (Acte I, Scène i, 87-8). With a religious twist as his distinguishing mark, Néarque represents the generation of men, like Don Diègue and Le Vieil Horace, who are misogynists. His advice for Polyeucte is based on his lack of knowledge, or dread of women. Unlike Polyeucte, he has never known a woman's love and he perceives woman as man's enemy: "Fuyez un ennemi qui sait votre défaut" (Acte I, Scène i, 104). Polyeucte does realize that by following Néarque to Christianity, he will have to give up part of himself, and he fears the consequences ("Je ne puis," Acte I, Scène i, 103), the most important one being Pauline's reaction to his indifference.

Pauline's fears for Polyeucte's safety fail to influence him. He is no longer devoted to her, and he refuses to listen to her: "Ce changement d'attitude choque Pauline, et d'autant plus que c'était, non par caprice, mais par tendresse pour son mari, qu'elle lui demandait de ne pas sortir."[240] As another critic suggests, the heroines are not compatible with the heroes: ". . . et qu'au sens ou elles prenaient le mot amour, elles sont seules à aimer. . . . Or les héroïnes de Corneille représentent d'abord cette capacité d'aimer autre chose que soi."[241] Pauline expresses her disillusionment at her fate as a woman, and also, "sur l'ingratitude des hommes du siècle":[242]

> Tu vois, ma Stratonice, en quel siècle nous sommes:
> Voilà notre pouvoir sur les esprits des hommes;
> . . . .
> Tant qu'ils ne sont qu'amants, nous sommes souveraines,
> Et jusqu'à la conquête ils nous traitent de reines;
> Mais après l'hyménée ils sont rois à leur tour.
> (Acte I, Scène iii, 129-30; 133-35)

At a point where the love interest seems to be growing weaker, Corneille injects new life into this theme by introducing a love triangle with the reappearance of Pauline's former suitor, Sévère. Love, and not politics, is the cause for Sévère's visit, in other words, the political element in the play seems secondary to the love element. For Doubrovsky, Sévère represents the lover, a permanent figure in Corneille's dramaturgy: ". . . Sévère est l'homme qui fait de l'amour humain sa divinité. . . ."[243] Lancaster presents another view of Sévère:

Sévère, as has often been pointed
out is the typical "honnête homme" of
the seventeenth century. Brave, loyal,
and devoted, he responds to the trust
that Pauline places in him and even
seeks at her request to save the man
who has come between them.[244]

Sévère's character appears to blend male and female
values in a harmonious and non-destructive fashion.
Sévère reappears on the scene to praise Pauline, the
woman he loves:

> Pourrai-je voir Pauline, et rendre
> à ses beaux yeux
> L'hommage souverain que l'on va rendre
> aux Dieux?
> . . . .
> Je viens sacrifier, mais c'est à ses
> beautés
> Que je viens immoler toutes mes
> volontés.
> (Acte II, Scène i, 367-68; 371-72)

Sévère's lines stress the importance of woman. He is
in Armenia to see Pauline and to find out if she still
loves him: "Mais ai-je sur son âme encor quelque
pouvoir? / . . . . Jamais à ses désirs mon coeur ne
fut rebelle" (Acte II, scène i, 375; 382). His
happiness is centered on Pauline: "Je n'aime mon
bonheur que pour la mériter" (Acte II, Scène i, 396).

Once Sévère discovers that Pauline is married, he
reacts with desperation: "Pauline, je verrai qu'un
autre vous possède!" (Acte II, Scène i, 422). He, as
the perfect lover, wants to see her, then die: "Je ne
veux que la voir, soupirer, et mourir" (Acte II,
Scène, 436). He still adores her and despite his
grave disappointment at losing her, he does not blame
her, he knows she had to marry someone else:

> Elle n'est point parjure, elle n'est
> point légère:
> Son devoir m'a trahi, mon malheur, et
> son père.
> Mais son devoir fut juste, et son père
> eut raison:
> J'impute à mon malheur toute la
> trahison.
> (Acte II, Scène i, 445-48)

Pauline's sense that Sévère would not blame her ("il est trop généreux," Acte I, Scène iv, 327) was accurate; however, Sévère's grief at having lost her: "Laisse-la-moi donc voir, soupirer, et mourir" (Acte II, Scène i, 452), is far more desperate than she possibly imagined. When Adam speaks of the emotional beauty of this play, it is no mistake that he focuses on the eventual Pauline/Sévère encounter: "Elle [l'émotion] éclate dans cette rencontre de Pauline et de Sévère, qui est sans doute l'un des sommets de la littérature de tous les temps."[245]

The central theme of Polyeucte appears to be the love theme. The love triangle, the rivalry between the two males for Pauline, the separated lovers caused by a forced marriage, the regrets based on a lost love, Pauline's anger at Polyeucte's indifference, all of these factors are part of the love element, which runs throughout the play. When Pauline angrily says to Polyeucte: "Tu préfères la mort à l'amour de Pauline!" (Acte IV, Scène iii, 1287), her tone is indignant and full of shock, indicating that Polyeucte has committed the worst of crimes; he has become indifferent to her love, and he denies all love that is tied to an earthly life. Polyeucte, like the Cornelian heroes before him, chooses either death, or confrontations with death that oppose the more human values of the heroines, the highest value being that of love for oneself and for others. The difference between heroine and hero is also based on the type of love each one manifests:

> Pourquoi s'étonner, dès lors que la femme qui s'en détache se veuille distincte du héros? Elle est distincte. Elle conçoit tout autrement l'amour, la gloire et l'heureux accomplissement personnel. L'amour que manifeste le héros demeure profondément narcissique; celui de l'héroïne s'adresse à un objet dont elle sépare nettement l'image de sa sienne propre; l'une des gloires tend à l'omnipotence, l'autre à la courtoisie; le héros s'accomplit dans la solitude, elle ne rêve que du couple, ne hait que la mutilation qui la prive du père ou de l'amant.[246]

What Mauron's psychocritical theories fail to include is the possibility for a type such as Sévère, who is closer to the heroine's characteristics.

One of Corneille's significant contributions is
that he elevated the status of the love element in
tragedy, and made a legitimate place for it there,
much to the delight of his audience. The presence of
the love element also adds an important alternative to
male heroics, which denies the preservation of
humanity--unlike the female ethic, which includes
human love. When Stegmann observes that: "Ce
triomphe de l'amour contribue fortement à la
détérioration de l'ancien idéal héroïque,"[247] he pits
the female ethic against the male ethic, which seems
inaccurate and counterproductive. Corneille himself,
presents the male ethic in an ambivalent manner:
"Corneille loved heroics, heady verse, and grand
gestures. But by listening hard, one detects notes of
anguish in his work, too, over the violence human
beings have done to themselves."[248] As we have seen
thus far, the violence in Corneille's tragedies
originates from and is committed by men. Corneille
wisely presents two views on life, which shows his
optimism, because the love element in the female
ethic, and the female ethic itself, is another human
alternative in life.

199. Harriet R. Allentuch, "Reflections on Women in the Theater of Corneille," Kentucky Romance Quarterly, 1974, vol. XXI, Number 1 (1974), p. 100.

200. Jean Louis Guez de Balzac, Letters: 27 aout 1637 and 17 janvier 1643, in Lettres Choisies Du Sieur De Balzac (Leiden: Chez les Elseviers, 1652).

201. Pierre Corneille, Discours du Poème Dramatique in Oeuvres de Pierre Corneille, Vol. I, ed. Charles Marty-Laveaux (Paris: Hachette, 1862), p. 24.

202. See the 1660 Examen of Le Cid in Oeuvres de Pierre Corneille, Vol. III, ed. Charles Marty-Laveaux (Paris: Hachette, 1862), p. 94.

203. Jacques Scherer, La Dramaturgie Classique en France (Paris: Librairie Nizet, 1950), p. 24.

204. Scherer, p. 25.

205. See Maurice Cauchie's edition of Le Cid (Paris: M. Didier, 1946), for original 1637 text which includes the original first scene of the play that was deleted because of the Académie's criticisms.

206. Georges Couton, Corneille (Paris: Hatier, 1969), p. 42.

207. Maurice Descotes, Les Grands Rôles du Théâtre de Corneille, p. 23.

208. Charles Ayer's theory that Corneille employed a second heroine in order to introduce the love element in his tragedies seems particularly accurate when judging L'Infante's role.

209. See Marie-Odile Sweetser, La Dramaturgie de Corneille (Paris: Droz, 1977), p. 114; André Stegmann, L'Héroïsme Cornélien, Vol. II (Paris: Armand Colin, 1968), p. 579.

210. Pierre Corneille, Discours du Poème Dramatique in Oeuvres de Pierre Corneille, Vol. I, ed. Charles Marty-Laveaux (Paris: Hachette, 1862), p. 48.

211. Georges Couton, Réalisme de Corneille: La Clef de Mélite; Réalités dans Le Cid (Paris: Société d'Edition "Les Belles Lettres," 1953), p. 92.

212. See Serge Doubrovsky, Corneille et la dialectique du héros (Paris: Gallimard, 1963), p. 99.

213. See the 1660 Examen of Le Cid in Oeuvres de Pierre Corneille, Vol. III, ed. Charles Marty-Laveaux (Paris: Hachette, 1862), p. 94.

214. Jacques Scherer, La Dramaturgie Classique en France, p. 30.

215. Charles Ayer, The Tragic Heroines of Corneille, p. 48.

216. Paul Bénichou, Morales du Grand Siècle. (Paris: Gallimard, 1948), p. 30.

217. Maurice Descotes, Les Grands Rôles du Théâtre de Corneille, p. 150.

218. Louis Herland, Horace ou Naissance de l'Homme. (Paris: Les Editions de Minuit, 1952), p. 41.

219. Charles Mauron, Des Métaphores Obsédantes au Mythe Personnel, p. 261.

220. Charles Ayer, The Tragic Heroines of Pierre Corneille, p. 83.

221. Ian MacLean, Woman Triumphant: Feminism in French Literature 1610-1652, p. 183.

222. Maria Tastevin, Les Héroïnes de Corneille, p. 57.

223. Henry Carrington Lancaster, A History of French Dramatic Literature . . . , p. 315; and Charles Ayer, The Tragic Heroines of Corneille, p. 28.

224. Claude Abraham, Pierre Corneille (New York: Twayne, 1978), p. 68.

225. Georges Couton, Corneille (Paris: Hatier, 1969), p. 64.

226. Voltaire, Commentaires sur Corneille (Paris: Firmin-Didot, 1800), p. 124.

227. Voltaire, p. 119.

228. Tastevin suggests that Cinna is more concerned about pleasing Emilie than winning male admiration (p. 76), while Allentuch actually discusses Cinna's inversion in, "The Problem of Cinna," The French Review, p. 881.

229. Serge Doubrovsky, Corneille et la dialectique du héros (Paris: Gallimard, 1963), p. 188.

230. Roger Lathuillère, La Préciosité. Etude Historique et Linguistique. Vol. I (Genève: Droz, 1966), p. 471.

231. Antoine Adam, Histoire de la Littérature Française, Vol. II (Paris: Editions Mondiales, 1962), p. 533.

232. Marie-Odile Sweetser, La Dramaturgie de Corneille, p. 119.

233. Doubrovsky, p. 197.

234. Charles C. Ayer, The Tragic Heroines of Pierre Corneille. (Strassburg: Heitz, 1898), p. 5. See also, Corneille's Examen of Polyeucte- in Charles-Marty-Laveaux, Oeuvres de Pierre Corneille, Vol. III, p. 481.

235. Allentuch, "Pauline and the Princesse de Clèves," MLQ, p. 172.

236. Maurice Descotes, Les grands Rôles du Théâtre de Corneille, p. 208.

237. Antoine Adam, Histoire de la Littérature Française, Vol. II. (Paris: Editions Mondiales, 1962), p. 540. See also, Claude Abraham, Pierre Corneille. (New York: Twayne, 1978), p. 73.

238. Critics who emphasize Corneille's marital status are: Adam, p. 541; Abraham, p. 73; Henry Carrington Lancaster, A History of French Dramatic Literature in the Seventeenth Century, p. 328; and Jean Schlumberger, Plaisir à Corneille (Paris: Gallimard, 1936), p. 93.

239. Adam, p. 541.

240. Maria Tastevin, Les Héroïnes de Corneille, p. 111.

241. Charles Mauron, _Des Métaphores Obsédantes au Mythe Personnel_, p. 262.

242. Tastevin, p. 111.

243. Doubrovsky, p. 235.

244. Lancaster, p. 327.

245. Antoine Adam, _Histoire de la Littérature Française_, Vol. II, p. 540.

246. Mauron, p. 253.

247. André Stegmann, _L'Héroisme Cornélien. Genèse et Signification_. Vol. II (Paris: Armand Colin, 1968), p. 569.

248. Harriet R. Allentuch, "Pauline and the Princesse de Clèves," _MLQ_, p. 182.

CHAPTER III

THE FATE OF THE HEROINE

The fate of the heroine at the dénouement of each play aids in gauging Corneille's perspective on them. As a dramatist, Corneille was an important innovator. His image of women is authentic,[249] both for his female protagonists who represent the political women of his time, and his other female characters whose behavior usually opposes that of the female protagonists. Through the examination of the fate of the heroine at the dénouement, we will see that the female characters who conform to the demands of patriarchal society are rewarded, whereas, the female protagonists will be silenced or rendered ineffective.

The fate of the heroine is also mirrored through the use of certain words that occur throughout the play,which are references <u>to</u> the heroine, therefore being indirect, or direct references made by the heroine to herself. The progression of these references mirrors the defeat of the female ethic by the male ethic. This progression of references will also indicate the extent to which the main heroine's assertion of her rights, is met with disapproval and censure.

Indirect or Direct Verbal References

In the <u>Stances</u>, Rodrigue refers to Chimène seven times. He even calls her "ma Chimène" which shows how deeply Rodrigue identified his happiness with the possession of Chimène. When Rodrigue refers to Chimène as "ma Chimène," perhaps, at this point in the play (Acte I, Scène vi), he is expressing how close he and Chimène were to being happy with each other; however, he thinks in terms of possessing Chimène as if she were his property. Chimène never refers to Rodrigue in possessive terms. In fact, from the beginning of the play, she realizes that their happiness is doomed. Yet, as late as during their first meeting (Acte III, Scène iv), Rodrigue still desires to possess Chimène, and again refers to her as "Ma Chimène." Despite the fact that he answered to the demands of his ethic, he seems to find no solace in it. His anguished emotions torture Chimène, overwhelm her with his needs, and ignore Chimène's need to act and defend her honor.

When the king orders that Chimène be put back in her house after she has demanded his justice: "Don Sanche, remettez Chimène en sa maison" (Acte II, Scène viii, 735), she reacts strongly to this dismissal. The fact that she must be "put back" in her house implies that her status is less significant than that of the males around her, and that she is treated like a child. Yet, Chimène resists being viewed as someone who can be dismissed and she defies the king: "M'ordonner du repos, c'est croître mes malheurs" (Acte II, Scène viii, 740). The last thing that Chimène needs is rest. She has a similar reaction to Elvire when she asks Chimène to rest: "Reposez-vous, Madame" (Acte III, Scène iii, 803). Chimène is outraged by the inappropriateness of this request: "Ah! que mal à propos / Dans un malheur si grand tu parles de repos!" (Acte III, Scène iii, 803-4). Once again, Chimène has a strong reaction to the word "repos" which contradicts the great effort she has to make to arouse all her moral energy to pursue Rodrigue.

It is significant for a feminist study that Chimène refers to herself as someone who is being forced to act in a certain way. When Elvire asks: "Pensez-vous le poursuivre?" (Acte III, Scène iii, 825), Chimène stresses how she feels forced to pursue Rodrigue:

> Ah! cruelle pensée!
> Et cruelle poursuite où je me vois forcée!
> Je demande sa tête, et crains de l'obtenir:
> Ma mort suivra la sienne, et je le veux punir!
> (Acte III, Scène iii, 825-28)

What she must do to defend her honor, will destroy both her and Rodrigue; nevertheless, the rigors of the male code of honor force her to do so. Elvire senses the unprecedented intentions of Chimène to pursue Rodrigue, and she urges her to give up her plans: "Quittez, quittez, Madame, un dessein si tragique; / Ne vous imposez point de loi si tyrannique" (Acte III, Scène iii, 829-30). Elvire's reference to Chimène stresses that the law or code she is following is self-imposed. Chimène is in control of her behavior, she is dictating to herself what she must do despite the painful consequences. It is unusual for a woman to decide to act and to have an equivalent sense of possibilities for her defense. Elvire's next reference to Chimène implies this: "Ne vous obstinez point en cette humeur étrange" (Acte III, Scène iii, 841). Chimène's behavior is considered bizarre and strange for her sex, and her intentions run counter to what is expected from her, which is to allow the king to act _for_ her.

The word "silence" changes meaning according to the speaker. Chimène's initial use of it equates silence with cowardly behavior or lack of courage:

> Quoi! mon père étant mort, et presque entre mes bras
> Son sang criera vengeance, et je ne l'orrai pas!
> Mon coeur, honteusement surpris par d'autres charmes,
> Croira ne lui devoir que d'impuissantes larmes
> Et je pourrai souffrir qu'un amour suborneur
> Sous un lâche silence étouffe mon honneur!
> (Acte III, Scène iii, 831-36)

She refuses to remain silent, in fact, silence contradicts all that she believes in. After Rodrigue's first forced entry (Acte III, Scène iv), Chimène refers to silence as something she needs after much emotional turmoil: "Je cherche le silence et la nuit pour pleurer" (Acte III, Scène iv, 1000). Chimène chooses a silence that connotes calm and stillness. She wishes to be alone so that she can grieve without any further intrusions.

When Don Diègue assures Rodrigue that he will possess Chimène again, once he has defended his country, he is working to reinspire military values in his son:

> . . . force par ta vaillance
> Ce monarque au pardon, et Chimène au silence;
> Si tu l'aimes, apprends que revenir vainqueur,
> C'est l'unique moyen de regagner son coeur.
> (Acte III, Scène vi, 1093-96)

Don Diègue refers to the forced silence that the king has required of Chimène, and that will be final, if Rodrigue returns as a hero. In Don Diègue's view of the world, Rodrigue's achievements in the public domain will permanently silence Chimène. It seems that everyone in the play is working to silence Chimène. The word "taire" is also used to refer to Chimène. Elvire uses it to express her outrage towards Chimène's resistance:

> Quoi! vous voulez encor refuser le bonheur
> De pouvoir maintenant vous taire avec honneur?
> . . . .
> Allez, dans le caprice où votre humeur s'obstine,
> Vous ne méritez pas l'amant qu'on vous destine;
>> (Acte V, Scène iv, 1687-88; 1693-94)

It is appropriate that such efforts are expended to silence Chimène, since words are her source of power.

The remaining references to Chimène in the play mirror the attempts to defeat her, or to show strong disapproval towards her. As Rodrigue tells the glorious stories of his victories, Chimène enters to demand justice (Acte IV, Scène iv). At this time, the king refers to Chimène's duty as being inopportune and intrusive:

> La fâcheuse nouvelle, et l'importun devoir!
> Va, je ne la veux pas obliger à te voir.
> Pour tous remerciements il faut que je te chasse
> Mais avant que sortir, viens, que ton roi t'embrasse.
>> (Acte IV, Scène iv, 1331-34)

The king considers the news of Chimène's reappearance as troublesome ("fâcheuse nouvelle"). These references to her indicate that her pursuit of Rodrigue will end in failure, since, in her case, duty takes on a negative connotation, because her demands are inconvenient to the king. Chimène's defeat at the end of the play is mirrored in the king's references to her, because her quest for honor is not taken seriously by the king.

140

It is ironic that the king equates Chimène's bold
determination with a type of violence: "Ma fille, ces
transports ont trop de violence" (Acte IV, Scène v,
1385). He equates her mere words with violence,
whereas we have seen the king find real physical
violence and bloodshed, Le Comte's death, for example,
justifiable. The king even belittles the veracity of
Chimène's words: ". . . il dit même brutalement à la
jeune fille qu'il ne croit pas à la sincérité de sa
supplique. . . ."250 Chimène must urge the king to
grant her justice. He finally agrees to a duel
between Don Sanche and Rodrigue to satisfy Chimène;
however, he is impatient with her and her demands:
"Choisis qui tu voudras, Chimène, et choisis bien; /
Mais après ce combat ne demande plus rien" (Acte IV,
Scène v, 1431-32). Chimène must marry the victor.
Despite her protest against the severe terms of the
duel: "Quoi! Sire, m'imposer une si dure loi!" (Acte
IV, Scène v, 1460), the king is firm. He is tired of
Chimène's demands and wishes her to be silent: "Cesse
de murmurer contre un arrêt si doux . . . / Qui que ce
soit des deux, j'en ferai ton époux" (Acte IV, Scène
v, 1463-64). It seems cruel that the king wants
Chimène to be silent since words are the only source
of her power. It is clear that Chimène's quest for
honor has been belittled and mocked by the king.

The last references to Chimène in the play
indicate that she will be silenced by the king's
ruling. Chimène is referred to as a rebel because she
has continually resisted the king's authority: "Et ne
sois point rebelle à mon commandement" (Acte V, Scène
vi, 1771). Yet, it does seem curious that Chimène is
called a rebel because she worked to satisfy her honor
through the king's justice. Her demands allowed her
to control her fate and not be forced to accept
authority that would cause hardships against her quest
for honor. The king's reference to her as a rebel
exaggerates Chimène's past willingness to work through
the king's justice.

At the dénouement of the play, Chimène is twice
referred to in monetary terms. She is the reward one
of the men will receive as the winner of the duel.
Chimène pleads with the king to revoke his ordinance:

> De grâce, révoquez une si dure loi;
> Pour prix d'une victoire où je perds ce
> que j'aime,
> Je lui laisse mon bien; qu'il me laisse
> à moi-même;

> Qu'en un cloître sacré je pleure
> incessamment,
> Jusqu'au dernier soupir, mon père et
> mon amant.
>
> (Acte V, Scène vi, 1736-40)

She does not wish to be transferred as the reward of a duel. Tastevin emphasizes the resigned tone in Chimène's voice, as she asks to be able to renounce this world and retreat to a convent: "Il faut noter tout ce qu'il y a déjà de résignation dans le ton de Chimène, lorsqu'elle s'adresse au roi."[251]

When Chimène questions the idea of a marriage between herself and Rodrigue, the winner of the duel, so soon after her father's death, she is objecting to the king's rigid ordinance. She doubts whether it is legitimate that she be considered the reward of the duel: "Si Rodrigue à l'Etat devient si nécessaire, / De ce qu'il fait pour vous dois-je être le salaire" (Acte V, Scène vii, 1809-10). She again objects to being equated with a reward; however, the king pays little attention to her objection: "Rodrigue t'a gagnée, et tu dois être à lui" (Acte V, Scène vii, 1815). The king continues to refer to Chimène in monetary terms ("gagnée), thus equating her with a possession that is rightfully Rodrigue's. These references make it clear that as a woman Chimène is considered male property. Yet, her resistance to being referred to this way will help her gain a one-year mourning period during which time all marriage plans will be suspended. Despite the references to Chimène that mirror that the patriarchal ethic will make her subordinate, Chimène resists it and attempts to control her own fate.

Camille, like Chimène, is in a position of forced dependency; her father has absolute power over her fate. Camille's first reference to herself indicates that she is subject to her father's authority and that he has the right to choose her marriage partner:

> Il vous souvient qu'à peine on
> voyoit de sa soeur
> Par un heureux hymen mon frère
> possesseur,
> Quand, pour comble de joie, il obtint
> de mon père
> Que de ses chastes feux je serois le
> salaire.
>
> (Acte I, Scène ii, 169-72)

142

Implicit in the last line: "Que de ses chastes feux je serois le salaire," is the notion of an exchange of one thing for another. Curiace's love for Camille will be rewarded. She will be the prize or compensation he will receive. Camille's reference to herself as, "le salaire" indicates her awareness of her fate as a woman. She knows that she is equivalent, in her father's mind, to a monetary reward which he can bestow on the man of his choosing.

When Curiace meets with Camille for the first time in the play (Acte I, Scène iii), he is hopeful for the success of their love and eventual marriage. He is confident that Camille's father approves of him and that their happiness is certain:

> Et mes desirs ont eu des succès si prospères,
> Que l'auteur de vos jours m'a promis à demain
> Le bonheur sans pareil de vous donner la main
> Vous ne deviendrez pas rebelle à sa puissance?
>   (Acte I, Scène iii, 336-39)

Curiace's reference to Camille as being "rebelle" is highly suggestive. We are given the first proof of Camille's resistant and rebellious spirit through this reference. Curiace has prepared the way for a characteristic of Camille that will become more pronounced as the play progresses.

When Camille refers to herself as a prize or reward ("prix"), she is shocked that she will be the subject of a male exchange. If Curiace is the victor of the duel, he will receive her hand in marriage as his payment. Camille is outraged by this fact: "Tu pourras donc, cruel, me présenter sa tête, / Et demander ma main pour prix de ta conquête!" (Acte II, Scène v, 567-68). She opposes the idea that after men battle to the death, they can return and claim a woman as their prize. Camille does not want to be in any way connected with male violence, that is why she reacts so strongly to being called a prize. She is also aware that the implication of this reference is that, as a woman, she is valued as property or as an exchangeable commodity.

Le Vieil Horace's references to women in Horace gives an idea of how low or devalued their status is

for his generation. When Horace and Curiace are
spending time with Sabine and Camille before the duel,
Le Vieil Horace is angry that they are not in battle
yet. He cannot believe that they are wasting time
with women: "Qu'est-ce-ci, mes enfants? écoutez-vous
vos flammes, / Et perdez-vous encor le temps avec des
femmes?" (Acte II, Scène vii, 679-80). He also fears
women's influence so soon before a battle, and
therefore, decides to confine them to their homes so
that they cannot interrupt the battle. Le Vieil
Horace is a man who believes that women should be
silent, or forced to be so. He silences Camille in
his impatience to learn of the results of the duel:
"Taisez-vous, et sachons ce que nous veut Valère"
(Acte IV, Scène i, 1071). He is an example of a male
in the play who is totally insensitive to women's
values, and assigns them a low status.

Camille's long, forced silence ends once Le Vieil
Horace exits and leaves her to the privacy of her
grief. Her revenge on her father, Horace, and the
male ethic, will begin. She feels that the reversals
in her fortune have been a type of slow pain. She
refers to herself as a plaything or a toy ("jouet") in
the hands of fate:

> En vit-on jamais un dont les rudes
> traverses
> Prissent en moins de rien tant de faces
> diverses,
> Qui fût doux tant de fois, et tant de
> fois cruel,
> Et portât tant de coups avant le coup
> mortel?
> Vit-on jamais une âme en un jour plus
> atteinte
> De joie et de douleur, d'espérance et
> de crainte,
> Asservie   en   esclave   à   plus
> d'événements,
> Et le pitieux jouet de plus de
> changements?
> Un oracle m'assure, un songe me
> travaille;
> (Acte IV, Scène iv, 1203-11)

Camille also compares herself to a slave who has been
forced to withstand so many changes of fate and so
much pain. These two references are important if we
are to understand Camille's revenge, its causes and

its effects on her, and her resistance against the male ethic in the play.

Despite Horace's victory, Camille can feel only grief at the loss of Curiace. She cannot greet him with joy over the murder of a loved one. She longs to be with Curiace. Horace is outraged that Camille still thinks of Curiace as her lover:

> O d'une <u>indigne</u> soeur <u>insupportable audace</u>!
> D'un ennemi public dont je reviens vainqueur
> Le nom est dans ta bouche et l'amour dans ton coeur!
> Ton ardeur <u>criminelle</u> à la vengeance aspire!
> Ta bouche la demande, et ton coeur la respire!
> (Acte IV, Scène v, 1268-72)

The underlined words (emphasis mine) stress that Camille, herself, is now considered a public enemy. She is unworthy ("indigne"), and she is also far too bold ("insupportable audace") for a woman. This is implied in Horace's indication of her sex ("soeur"). Her boldness cannot be tolerated by him. Horace perceives her as an enemy of Rome and she, like Curiace, will be destroyed. Camille's words are the only possible weapon she can use. Horace states that he is going to punish her because of her mouth. Although she is unarmed Horace kills her in cold blood. Horace becomes his sister's assassin, yet, considers her in abstract terms, and believes that he has destroyed another Roman enemy. He thinks he had the right to kill her as a result:

> Ne me dis point qu'elle est et mon sang et ma soeur.
> Mon père ne peut plus l'avouer pour sa fille:
> Qui maudit son pays renonce à sa famille;
> . . . .
> Et ce souhait impie, encore qu'impuissant,
> Est un monstre qu'il faut étouffer en naissant.
> (Acte IV, Scène vi, 1326-28; 1333-34)

145

Camille's wish to be with Curiace is compared to a monster that must perish. This last reference also implies that Camille is a monster, which is ironic. Camille espoused human love as a supreme value, and she is deemed unfit for a world dominated by brutality and violence.

Emilie's first reference to herself occurs in the expression, "la fille d'un proscrit," which has a very strong and derogatory meaning for her. Despite Auguste's adoption of Emilie, she is haunted and oppressed by her status as the daughter of an outcast. Her hatred for Auguste has been nourished by the painful memory of her father's banished status and murder; and the hate that she unleashes against Auguste is the result of it. Since Emilie never knew her father, the fuel for her hatred comes directly from the power of her memory,[252] and from her sense of being marked by her father's disgrace, which she must avenge.

Emilie's confidante, Fulvie, urges Emilie to diminish the forcefulness of her desire to kill Auguste: "Mais encore une fois souffrez que je vous die / Qu'une si juste ardeur devroit être attiédie" (Acte I, Scène ii, 62-3). Fulvie tries to make Emilie dilute or lessen her drive to conspire against Auguste. Fulvie also suggests that she will be considered an ingrate, if she does not abandon her hatred for Auguste: "Quel besoin toutefois de passer pour ingrate?" (Acte I, Scène ii, 85-6). Emilie ignores both of these warnings because she has no faith in Auguste's favors, and disregards them because they are based on a false foundation of violence and crime. Fulvie's references to Emilie has no real power over her imagination.

The word "prix," when referring to the heroine, has two distinct meanings according to the sex of the speaker. When Emilie refers to herself as a "prix," it takes on an affective, "précieux" meaning, as is illustrated when she speaks to her lover, Cinna: "Souviens-toi du beau feu dont nous sommes épris, / Qu'aussi bien que la gloire Emilie est ton prix" (Acte I, Scène iii, 275-76). Cinna will receive Emilie as a reward for his service and love; Emilie will freely give her love to Cinna. However, in the male vocabulary, "prix" takes on a military meaning, as has already been seen in Le Cid and Horace. Heroines are referred to in monetary terms, when they are being passed from one male to another. There are two

incidents in the play where Auguste rewards Cinna by
promising Emilie in exchange for his loyalty to the
emperor. Emilie is shocked when she discovers that
Cinna believes in Auguste's munificence, and that he
can give her to Cinna:

> Et ton esprit crédule ose s'imaginer
> Qu'Auguste, pouvant tout, peut aussi me
> donner.
> Tu me veux de sa main plutôt que de la
> mienne.
> (Acte III, Scène iv, 935-37)

Emilie's shock becomes outrage when she realizes that
Cinna has been influenced by Auguste: "Que je sois le
butin de qui l'ose épargner, / Et le prix du conseil
qui le force à regner!" (Acte III, Scène iv, 959-60),
and that Cinna and Auguste believe that she can be
exchanged from one male to the next, as if she were
owned, like booty after a war.

It is also possible to gauge Cinna's deepening
distance from Emilie, as a result of a few of his
references to her. Cinna's weakening loyalty to
Emilie is apparent in this reference: "Mais voici de
retour cette aimable inhumaine" (Acte III, Scène iii,
905). Although Cinna still loves Emilie, he believes
that she is asking too much of him. In his eyes, love
is also deemed inhuman: "Mais l'empire inhumain
qu'exercent vos beautés / Force jusqu'aux esprits et
jusqu'aux volontés" (Acte III, Scène iv, 1055-56), and
Emilie's love is tyrannical: "Mais apprenez
qu'Auguste est moins tyran que vous" (Acte III, Scène
iv, 1052). Emilie, who must depend on Cinna for
direct action against Auguste, is losing her foothold.
Auguste's munificence has already taken precedence
over Cinna's love for Emilie. By Act III, it is
evident through Cinna's references to her, that she
will not have the vengeance she desires, and that
Cinna is increasingly more detached from her.[253]

Auguste's references to Emilie indicate his
disapproval of her behavior. Once Auguste knows about
the conspiracy he considers Emilie unworthy of all
that he has done for her: "Et je la vois comme elle
indigne de ce rang" (Acte V, Scène ii, 1591). His
reference to Emilie as being unworthy is a sign of
Auguste's strong reaction to what is actually Emilie's
indifference to him. Auguste's next reference to
Emilie seems ironic, since it is coming from a ruler
who gained access to power through many murderous and

violent acts: "L'une fut impudique, et l'autre est parricide" (Acte V, Scène ii, 1594). Auguste is implying that Emilie is a parricide because she intends to kill him, her adoptive father. This accusation is meaningless to Emilie since the only man she considered to be her father was murdered by Auguste.

By the dénouement of the play, Emilie remains consistent in her demands for vengeance, but the references to her indicate that Emilie becomes isolated from the other characters because her demands are thought to be unreasonable and against the good of Rome. Emilie's behavior is considered socially unacceptable. Corneille puts the final words of disapproval in Livie's mouth, who, as another female, is regarded as being more socially acceptable. It is Livie who silences Emilie:

> C'en est trop, Emilie: arrête, et considère
> Qu'il t'a trop bien payé les bienfaits de ton père:
> Sa mort, dont la mémoire allume ta fureur,
> Fut un crime d'Octave, et non de l'Empereur,
> Tous ces crimes d'Etat qu'on fait pour la couronne,
> Le ciel nous en absout qu'il nous la donne.
> (Acte V, Scène ii, 1605-10)

These words confirm the outcome of all the references: that Emilie would be silenced and forced to renounce her hatred of Auguste. The fact that Livie silences Emilie signifies that Emilie's behavior is not approved of by society, and that Corneille concurs with that reality.

After Félix learns that Sévère is still alive, his reference to Pauline's "rebellion" stresses the fact that she did not obey Félix without protest:

> Ah! Pauline, en effet, tu m'as trop obéi;
> Ton courage étoit bon, ton devoir l'a trahi.
> Que ta rébellion m'eût été favorable!

> Qu'elle m'eût garanti d'un état
> déplorable.
>   (Acte I, Scène iv, 331-34)

As we learned from Pauline's rejection of parental authority, she was deeply hurt by Félix's failure to allow Sévère and her to marry. Her rebellion against Félix's unreasonable demands is complete by the dénouement (Acte V, Scène ii and Scène v).

When Félix makes another unreasonable demand on her, that she see Sévère, Pauline refers to herself as a victim: "Oui, je vais de nouveau dompter mes sentiments, / Pour servir de victime à vos commandements" (Acte I, Scène iv, 363-64). She has already learned by obeying Félix that she is not being guided wisely. She knows the risks involved for herself; however, she obeys him now because his political fortunes and hers, through association with him, depend on her success with Sévère: "Et songe qu'en tes mains tu tiens nos destinées" (Acte I, Scène iv, 362).

Sévère's initial references to Pauline indicate that he still loves her, is still possibly hopeful for their love, and has much admiration for her:

> Ainsi de vos desirs toujours reine
> absolue,
> Les plus grands changements vous
> trouvent résolue;
> De la plus forte ardeur vous portez vos
> esprits
> Jusqu'à l'indifférence et peut-être au
> mépris;
> Et votre fermeté fait succéder sans
> peine
> La faveur au dédain, et l'amour à la
> haine.
>   (Acte II, Scène ii, 481-86)

Sévère is observing Pauline with the eyes of a devoted lover, yet, his feelings of regret soon follow his praise.

Pauline refers to herself as being governed by the laws of a man: "Et qui me range ici dessous les lois d'un homme" (Acte II, Scène ii, 514), which ties in with her earlier reference to herself as a victim. She makes it clear to Sévère that she is not acting according to her own will, but that she is forced to

149

obey her father. It is obvious that Pauline has
little tangible power over her fate. When Polyeucte
falls from favor with Félix, after his conversion to
Christianity, Félix orders Pauline to stop bothering
him, and to try to influence Polyeucte:

> Vous m'importunez trop: bien que j'aye
> un coeur tendre,
> Je n'aime la pitié qu'au prix que j'en
> veux prendre;
> . . . .
> Allez: n'irritez plus un père qui vous
> aime,
> Et tâchez d'obtenir votre époux de
> lui-même.
> (Acte III, Scène iv, 979-98;
> 985-86)

Félix reveals himself as a political opportunist and
his daughter, Pauline, is useful to him insofar as she
is capable of doing what he wants.

Polyeucte's reference to Pauline as an
"obstacle," during his Stances indicate that she is
his last earthly tie, which obstructs his desire to
die as a martyr, and prove his love for God: "Et je
ne regarde Pauline / Que comme un obstacle à mon bien"
(Acte IV, Scène ii, 1143-44). Pauline is no longer
seen as a woman he loves but as a non-Christian, whose
lack of grace could possibly be changed in the future:
"Sur votre aveuglement il repandra le jour" (Acte IV,
Scène iii, 1266).

Pauline, in turn, makes two references to
Polyeucte, which are interesting to note, because they
imply an inversion of the sexes. We have seen that
Camille and Emilie have been referred to as being
ungrateful or cruel. In Polyeucte, Pauline will
accuse Polyeucte of being an ingrate; "Tu me quittes,
ingrat, et le fais avec joie" (Acte IV, Scène iii,
1247), when he demonstrates how little her love means
to him, because he has chosen religion over love.
Heroines are usually referred to as ingrates if they
refuse to obey a male authority figure. Pauline will
also refer to Polyeucte as being cruel, because he is
totally unmoved by her love: "Que t'ai-je fait,
cruel, pour être ainsi traitée" (Acte V, Scène iii,
1595). An inversion does occur in Polyeucte because
these epithets have thus far been reserved for the
heroines.

Sévère's reference to Pauline as a "présent" stresses the equivalence existing between a woman, and an object of exchange such as money. Pauline is equivalent to a material good when Polyeucte wishes her to live with Sévère as her husband once Polyeucte is dead. Sévère expresses his surprise at this desire: "Il en fait un présent lui-même à son rival!" (Acte IV, Scène v, 1322). What is clear from this reference is that Pauline is equivalent to property.

Sévère's final reference to Pauline, after she has asked him to try to save her husband, is that she is "inhumaine." It seems inappropriate that Sévère refer to Pauline in lover's terms, because Pauline has clearly stated that there is no possibility for their love to continue. Sévère cannot understand why he is no longer seen as a lover by her:

> Votre belle âme est haute autant que malheureuse,
> Mais elle est inhumaine autant que généreuse,
> Pauline, et vos douleurs avec trop de rigueur
> D'un amant tout à vous tyrannisent le coeur.
> (Acte IV, Scène v, 1379-82)

And the fact that he persists in thinking in these terms, indicates that he has not fully understood the nature of Pauline's moral struggles.

The Dénouement

As Act IV begins, Chimène realizes that her pursuit of Rodrigue will be more difficult now that he has risen to the level of a national hero. Yet, her demand for vengeance continues as she stirs up all of her moral energy for the battle ahead:

> Reprenons donc aussi ma colère affoiblie:
> Pour avoir soin de lui faut-il que je m'oublie?
> On le vante, on le loue, et mon coeur y consent!
> Mon honneur est muet, mon devoir impuissant!
> Silence, mon amour, laisse agir ma colère:

151

S'il a vaincu deux rois, il a tué mon
père.
(Acte IV, Scène i, 1125-30)

Chimène does not lose sight of the revenge she must
seek for her father's death. She overcomes her love
and lets her anger take over. Although Tastevin
indicates that Chimène's struggle is difficult, she
fails to perceive Chimène's anger in the following
interpretation:

> Et la lutte recommence dans son
> pauvre coeur déchiré, entre l'amour
> qu'elle veut faire taire et le devoir
> qu'elle s'est imposé. Elle s'excite de
> son mieux à la vengeance, elle se
> rappelle la mort de son père et cherche
> dans la vue de ses habits de deuil, de
> ses violes lugubres, un secours contre
> sa passion.[254]

Tastevin seems to pity Chimène for some reason, while
Chimène herself does not indulge in any self-pity.
Chimène is lucid about what she feels she must do, and
she lets her anger fuel her plans for revenge.

Despite the seriousness of Chimène's intentions
to seek revenge against Rodrigue, she will be
subjected to a cruel trick by the king. The king
plans to trick Chimène because he believes that her
pursuit of Rodrigue is merely a hoax. He assumes that
as a female, Chimène considers her love to be more
important than her need for revenge. This is implied
in a brief conversation between Don Diègue and the
king:

> Don Diègue: Chimène le poursuit, et
> voudrait le sauver.
> Don Fernand: On m'a dit qu'elle
> l'aime, et je vais
> l'éprouver.
> Montrez un oeil plus
> triste.
> (Acte IV, Scène iv, 1335-37)

When Chimène enters (Acte IV, Scène v), the king goes
along with his plan and tricks Chimène into believing
that Rodrigue is dead. Chimène faints from the news
and both the king and Don Diègue are convinced that
her love is really all that she is concerned about.
Don Diègue best expresses the only aspect of Chimène

that both he and the king take seriously:

> Mais voyez qu'elle pâme, et d'un amour
> parfait,
> Dans cette pâmoison, Sire, admirez
> l'effet.
> Sa douleur a trahi les secrets de son
> âme,
> Et ne vous permet plus de douter de sa
> flamme.
> (Acte IV, Scène v, 1343-46)

After all the struggle Chimène has gone through to make the king recognize the demands of her honor, she is ridiculed and humiliated. Mockery is her only reward.

In addition to the king's trick, a second trick will be played on Chimène. After the first trick which took Chimène by surprise, and caused her to experience a painful shift of emotions, the king then tells her that Rodrigue is really alive: "Non, non, il voit le jour, / Et te conserve encore un immuable amour" (Acte IV, Scène v, 1347-48). Tastevin notes the emotional gymnastics that Chimène experiences because of the king's cruel trick:

> Le monarque emploie d'abord une ruse
> atroce en lui annonçant à l'improviste
> la mort de Rodrigue. L'émotion de
> Chimène est trop violente pour qu'elle
> puisse la dissimuler, et elle perd
> ainsi, dès le début, tous ses moyens.
> Cruellement, le roi note la douleur
> qu'elle a laissé paraître.[255]

The fact that Chimène's long struggle to defend her honor ends in ridicule and mockery, indicates that the seriousness of her demands were never taken in earnest by the king. The king has assumed that as a woman, love and not honor, is her predominant concern. This assumption is one frequently associated with the misogyny present in the views on women held by the older generation in Corneille's plays. Yet, what the king fails to grasp about Chimène's psychology, is best expressed by Nelson: "Chimène was not 'dissimulating' her love, but overcoming it."[256]

Chimène again unleashes her anger and expresses her outrage at the king. She is angry because she has been ridiculed and she has not been taken seriously:

153

"De ma juste poursuite on fait si peu de cas / Qu'on me croit obliger en ne m'écoutant pas!" (Acte IV, Scène v, 1395-96). She is aware that her demands have not really been heard by the king. She confronts the fact that she has been ignored with new demands. Chimène wants Rodrigue to pay for her father's death. After more demands made against Rodrigue's life, the king agrees to another duel (Acte IV, Scène v). Chimène is not happy with the terms of the duel: she must marry the victor, yet, she has the gratification that she has defended her honor in spite of all the obstacles presented before her.

Throughout the remainder of the play, Chimène will consistently resist the king's authority and refuse to be forced to marry Rodrigue. She is aware that Rodrigue chose his honor over his love: "Ton honneur t'est plus cher que je ne te suis chère, / Puisqu'il trempe tes mains dans le sang de mon père" (Acte V, Scène i, 11509-10). All Chimène wants is a chance for an equal battle: "Va, sans vouloir mourir, laisse-moi te poursuivre / Et défends ton honneur, si tu veux plus vivre" (Acte V, Scène i, 1521-22). Despite the fact that a duel is taking place between Don Sanche and Rodrigue (Acte V, Scène iv), Chimène is not satisfied and she bemoans the irreparable damage that has been done to her:

> Quoi! l'objet de ma haine ou de tant de colère!
> L'assassin de Rodrigue ou celui de mon père!
> De tous les deux côtés on me donne un mari
> Encor tout teint du sang que j'ai le plus chéri;
> De tous les deux côtés mon âme se rebelle:
> (Acte V, Scène iv, 1657-61)

She cannot accept a murderer for her husband. These lines also express Chimène's discomfort with an ethic that is dominated by bloodshed and violence.

Chimène's resistance and refusal to be forced to marry Rodrigue is clearly articulated in Act V, Scene iv. She will not allow herself to be coerced into a marriage that will compromise her honor:

> Quand il sera vainqueur, crois-tu que je me rende?

Mon devoir est trop fort, et ma perte
trop grande;
. . . .
Il peut vaincre don Sanche avec fort
peu de peine,
Mais non pas avec lui la gloire de
Chimène;
Et quoi qu'à sa victoire un monarque
ait promis,
Mon honneur lui fera mille autres
ennemis.
                    (Acte V, Scène iv, 1677-78;
1681-84)

Chimène remains consistent throughout the dénouement;
she resists the king's ordinance to marry Rodrigue
immediately after his victory over Don Sanche. She
also manages to bargain for a one-year mourning period
before her marriage can take place. Perhaps the lines
where Chimène states what she really wants her fate to
be are: "Que'en un cloître sacré je pleure
incessamment, / Jusqu'au dernier soupir, mon père et
mon amant" (Acte V, Scène vi, 1739-40). She would
like to leave behind all the suffering the world has
caused her and spend the rest of her life in a
cloister.[257]   Yet, the king has determined another
fate for her. She will marry Rodrigue because he has
rightfully won ("Rodrigue t'a gagnée. . . .") her in a
duel. It is not surprising that Chimène's fate at the
dénouement is difficult to determine in definite
terms. The dominant authority in the play, the king,
declares that Chimène shall be Rodrigue's wife, but
Chimène clearly wants no part of this marriage. She
would prefer to retreat from this world altogether.

Act IV, Scene iv marks the beginning of Camille's
revenge against a cruel father and the harsh world he
and Horace represent. Camille perceives her father as
her torturer; however, she rebels against his
unreasonable authority and refuses to be victimized by
him:

Qui, je lui ferai voir, par
d'infaillibles marques,
Qu'un véritable amour brave la main des
Parques,
Et ne prend point de lois de ces cruels
tyrans
Qu'un astre injurieux nous donne pour
parents.
Tu blâmes ma douleur, tu l'oses nommer

155

lâche;
Je l'aime d'autant plus que plus elle
te fâche,
Impitoyable père, et par un juste
effort
Je la veux rendre égale aux rigueurs de
mon sort.
                (Acte IV, Scène iv, 1195-1202)

Le Vieil Horace has been repeatedly insensitive to her
needs. She is certain that she has the right to mourn
her dead lover. As a result, she plans to offend
Horace in the same way he has offended her. This is
her plan of action:

Pour ce cruel vainqueur n'ayez point de
respect;
Loin d'éviter ses yeux, croissez à son
aspect;
Offensez sa victoire, irritez sa
colère,
Et prenez, s'il se peut, plaisir à lui
déplaire.
Il vient: préparons-nous à montrer
constamment
Ce que doit une amante à la mort d'un
amant.
                (Acte IV, Scène iv, 1245-50)

She will have her revenge against Horace and direct
her anger and grief against him.

When Horace greets Camille he expects her to
share the joy of his victory. He is completely
ignorant of her grief, which is not surprising,
because she has been forced to suppress natural
feelings for so long. Instead of sharing Horace's
victory, she demands that Curiace be returned to her:

Rends-moi mon Curiace, ou laisse agir
ma flamme:
Ma joie et mes douleurs dépendoient de
son sort;
Je l'adorais vivant, et je le pleure
mort.
                (Acte IV, Scène v, 1280-82)

Camille no longer considers herself Horace's sister;
and she threatens to pursue him until he kills her:

> Ne cherche plus ta soeur où tu
> l'avois laissée;
> Tu ne revois en moi qu'une amante
> offensée,
> Qui comme une furie attachée à tes pas,
> Te veut incessamment reprocher son
> trépas.
>
> (Acte IV, Scène v, 1283-86)

This, in effect, is Camille's challenge against her chief adversary in the play. After Camille curses Rome to Horace's face (Acte IV, scène v, 1301-18), he murders her in a fit of rage.

Much discussion surrounds Horace's murder of Camille; however, it is disconcerting that a majority of Cornelian critics justify Horace's act by blaming Camille for her own death. This is the case with Doubrovsky's interpretation:

> Dans le duel de l'homme et de la femme,
> le plus fort, dès qu'il emploie la
> force, s'avilit; le bras qui frappe
> n'est plus celui d'un héros, mais d'un
> assassin. Camille le sait et en
> profite.[258]

Although Doubrovsky understands that Horace not only degrades himself by using physical force against a woman, and that as a result, he is an assassin, his concluding sentence suddenly reverses the preceding evidence and lays the blame on Camille. In a conclusion that is a non sequitur, Doubrovsky finds Camille responsible for her own death. Abraham, in another vein, thinks that Camille deserved death because she was a threat to Rome:

> Camille, in attacking him, attacks Rome
> as well. . . . On this level of
> national policy, the right or wrong of
> Camille's death is not so much a matter
> of verdict as of execution: insofar as
> Camille attacked Rome, she deserved
> death, and her death was the result of
> a "reasonable" act.[259]

Abraham perceives Camille in the same light as Horace because he considers Camille a criminal and public enemy of Rome. It is clear that both Doubrovsky and Abraham manage to appreciate Horace's motivation and reason for killing Camille; yet, they completely fail

157

to examine the circumstances leading up to her death
from Camille's point of view. This is perhaps one of
the most basic proofs of male bias in criticism, which
is a failure to examine dramatic situations from the
point of view of both characters involved.

Both D'Aubignac and Lancaster find Corneille
responsible for Camille's murder. D'Aubignac wished
that Corneille made Camille run into Horace's sword so
as to prevent him from falling to the status of a
hero-assassin.[260] While Lancaster believes that
Corneille shows his indifference to the "Querelle du
Cid," and the unethical behavior of his heroines, by
allowing Camille's murder in his play:

> Moreover, Corneille's new play would
> serve to show his indifference to the
> criticism of Chimène's conduct as
> unethical, for it is certainly less in
> accord with commonly accepted morals to
> kill one's sister than to marry the
> murderer of one's father.[261]

In other words, instead of creating heroines who
respect the "bienséances," Corneille persists in
characterizing heroines as strong and rebellious
individuals. Tastevin is the only critic who attempts
to interpret Camille's murder from Camille's point of
view, or an approximation of it:

> Horace l'emporte parce qu'il a la force
> physique brutale; mais Camille est
> moralement invaincue. Elle tombe,
> aussi éperdûment éprise de Curiace,
> aussi affamée de vengeance contre Rome
> qu'elle l'a jamais été.[262]

Tastevin describes, in precise terms, the essential
conflict between Horace and Camille, which is between
brutality and morality. Horace espouses a destructive
male ethic that even allows him to kill his own
sister, while Camille remains consistent and morally
intact through her belief in human love and its worth.
If we examine Camille's murder from the perspective of
her beliefs and struggle, it appears that Camille is
the victim of a brutal and senseless act, and that the
one to blame is Horace, her assassin.

If Camille is the heroine who must perish at the
end of the play, Sabine is the one who survives.
Before the duel actually takes place, Horace tells

Curiace that he will talk to Sabine and that he will convince her to see things his way (Acte II, Scène iii, 511-14). He believes that Sabine will be his ally and observe her wifely duties. He feels that she will support his choices and continue to be his pious wife: "The message is made explicit, and this pious wife is shown as a moral example to the audience, and to all women."[263] Sabine is the heroine who survives in a male world because she is no real threat to it. Sabine realizes this to some extent when she says: "Que Camille est heureuse! elle a pu te déplaire;" (Acte IV, Scène vii, 1380). Although Sabine wishes to have a death similar to Camille's, she is allowed to survive. Sabine, like Chimène, finds herself bound to a man who is the murderer of a close relative:

> La mort que je demande, et qu'il faut que j'obtienne,
> Augmentera sa peine, et finira la mienne.
> . . . .
> Quelle horreur d'embrasser un homme dont l'épée
> De toute ma famille a la trame coupée!
> (Acte V, Scène iii, 1611-12; 1615-16)

Sabine deplores Horace's act and her fate as the wife of a murderer. Yet, Sabine is urged by Le Vieil Horace to observe her wifely duties (Acte V, Scène iii, 1644-46), and Horace is absolved of his crime. She is ordered to overcome her "weakness" and to act in a way that makes her worthy of her brothers:

> Sabine, écoutez moins la douleur qui vous presse;
> Chassez de ce grand coeur ces marques de foiblesse:
> C'est en séchant vos pleurs que vous vous montrerez
> La véritable soeur de ceux que vous pleurez.
> (Acte V, Scène iii, 1767-70)

Sabine is forced to accept male values, she is outnumbered and has no choice.

The final act of restitution is a joint burial for Camille and Curaice: 'Je veux qu'un même jour, témoin de leurs deux morts, / En un même tombeau voie enfermer leurs corps" (Acte V, Scène iii, 1781-82).

159

The political break between Alba and Rome is healed by
this symbolic gesture: "Enfin, la réconciliation
entre Rome et Albe résoudra le conflit initial et sera
symbolisée par la réunion de Camille et de Curiace
dans le même tombeau."[264] But the issues involved in
Camille's revolt against the male ethic and its
brutality are never resolved and even forgotten. As
Catharine Stimpson observes in a comparison between
tragic heroes and heroines:

> A tragic hero tends to have
> worldly power, the ability to influence
> people and events. Oedipus was, after
> all, a king. Thus, when heroes fall,
> when they commit a tragic error, they
> bring a world down with them. . . .
> When women are tragic heroines,
> however, they tend to fall alone.[265]

This is clearly the case with Camille and her revolt
against the male ethic.

When Emilie and Auguste confront each other for
the first time in the play, it is after the discovery
of the conspiracy. Livie leads Emilie into Auguste's
chambers and announces Emilie's guilt. Here, one
woman is leading another woman into a place where
women are rarely seen. Emilie, who had prepared
herself for the event of discovery, is ready for this
confrontation with Auguste. To the shock of Cinna and
Auguste, Emilie takes full blame for the conspiracy.
She asserts herself against Auguste and displays her
courage: "Qui, tout ce qu'il a fait, il l'a fait pour
me plaire, / Et j'en étois, Seigneur, la cause et le
salaire" (Acte V, Scène ii, 1565-66). Emilie states
that she made Cinna swear that he would kill Auguste.
She is ready to accept all the consequences of her
act. She is prepared to die and expects no pardon
from Auguste, least of all clemency: "Mourir en sa
présence, et rejoindre mon père, / C'est tout ce qui
m'amène, et tout ce que j'espère" (Acte V, Scène ii,
1585-86). In addition to this powerful assertion,
Emilie insists that she will continue to conspire
against Auguste, and that she will find other men to
serve her cause. Harriet Allentuch points out that a
remarkable characteristic of Cornelian heroines,
particularly in the tragedies, is: "A desire to be
judged by the same standards as men."[266] This is the
case with Emilie, who is ready to accept whatever
punishment befits her crime.

After such difficult statements, Emilie is outraged that Cinna contradicts her concerning her role as leader of the conspiracy. Not only does Cinna try to undercut everything Emilie asserts, but he also ridicules her along sexual lines to dissuade Auguste from believing her:

> Que la vengeance est douce à l'esprit
> d'une femme!
> . . . .
> Elle n'a conspiré que par mon artifice;
> J'en suis le seul auteur, elle n'est
> que complice.
> (Acte V, Scène ii, 1633; 1637-38)

A tug of war ensues between Cinna and Emilie over glory, which marks the presence of a comic rather than tragic mode in the dénouement. This comic tone has sad repercussions for Emilie because the beauty of her act against Auguste is undercut, devalued, and given little credibility. The problem remains that Emilie is subject to this type of ridicule because she had to act through Cinna. As Allentuch remarks: "But the stumbling block is always the same: women are denied the possibility of direct action."[267]

However, as has been evident thus far, Emilie is not a heroine who compromises her beliefs, or allows herself to be compromised by others, including her lover. She fights for equality with Cinna in the conspiracy. She insists that as true lovers, they should be equal in crime:

> Eh bien! prends-en ta part, et me
> laisse la mienne;
> Ce seroit l'affoiblir que d'affoiblir
> la tienne:
> La gloire et le plaisir, la honte et
> les tourments,
> Tout doit être commun entre de vrais
> amants.
> . . . .
> Vous vouliez nous unir, ne nous séparez
> pas.
> (Acte V, Scène ii, 1645-48; 1656)

Emilie asserts her right to equality with Cinna in crime. Her demands are successful, and she is able to gain credibility with Auguste because he now refers to them as a "couple ingrat." Despite Cinna's attempt to undercut her role in the conspiracy, Emilie is at least able to retain an equal status with Cinna in crime. Emilie remains consistent in her role in the conspiracy, but she threatens to continue to pursue Auguste for his past crimes.

What is actually Auguste's conversion has been dubbed by many critics as Emilie's conversion.[268] Lanson is convinced that Emilie suddenly changes at the end of the play: "tout d'un coup elle s'aperçoit que cet homme n'est plus le tyran qui méritait sa vengeance; elle sent tout son être changé."[269] Stegmann sees Emilie's conversion as a surprise; however, it makes the dénouement possible: ". . . seule la surprenante 'conversion' d'Emilie peut accorder les ennemis."[270] Doubrovsky, who also believes in Emilie's conversion, finds that Emilie is convinced of the necessity of the monarchy, and that her conversion to monarchy permits Auguste's triumph.[271] A more recent critique devoted exclusively to Emilie's conversion, never questions the notion of conversion per se, but it does stress that Emilie never denies her feelings of hatred for Auguste.[272] This interpretation is contradictory because Emilie's conversion is accepted as a given, yet it maintains that Emilie never changes throughout the play, as far as her hatred for Auguste is concerned.

Although Sweetser does accept the notion of Emilie's conversion, she stresses that Emilie freely accepts a reconciliation with Auguste, and that she is not forced to change.[273] While Tastevin, who never refers to Emilie's conversion, suggests that it is Auguste who changes suddenly ("La soudaineté de sa résolution surprend Emilie.").[274] It appears rather that her hatred dissipates because of Auguste's magnanimity, which seems to be totally out of character for him.

The theory of Emilie's conversion seems misplaced and inaccurate, because Emilie's behavior and goals remain consistent throughout the play. It seems much more accurate to refer to Auguste's sudden change in character in terms of a conversion as Allentuch has done: "Auguste's 'conversion,' his self-restraint and assumption of a new kind of imperial authority . . . provokes imitation by Emilie who also readjusts her character and ends the hostility between the principal characters."[275] Auguste is the character who converts, because his choice of clemency as a solution represents a rejection of his violent past. He

implores Emilie to take his example in order to avoid
further bloodshed. She can accept an option to avoid
any further bloodshed; and has satisfied her desire to
avenge her father's death, and she did not fail to
pursue her goals, despite the discovery of the
conspiracy:

> Elle sacrifie si complètement sa vie
> qu'elle ne s'irrite même pas de voir
> l'entreprise échouer à la dernière
> minute. Elle a tenté tout le possible
> pour son père et pour Rome, elle est
> satisfaite.[276]

Auguste's conversion is only half of what makes
the dénouement possible. The importance of Emilie's
willingness to renounce her hatred for Auguste should
not be underestimated. In fact, as Lancaster
suggests, Livie is actually responsible for the
dénouement since she advised Auguste to be clement
toward the conspirators.[277] Emilie's acceptance of
Auguste's clemency is what makes a bloodless
dénouement possible. She is the first to reply to
Auguste's clemency (Acte V, Scène iii, 1715-28) by
accepting his conversion, and by promising that her
hatred will subside. Although Livie's prophecy
indicates that the gods are in favor of Auguste's
clemency, it seems that Emilie and Livie make a happy
ending possible since the former agrees to renounce
her hatred for Auguste and avoid any further
bloodshed, while the latter advises Auguste (Acte IV,
Scène iii) to practice clemency on the conspirators.
The importance of the heroines in bringing about the
possibility of a happy ending for what was about to be
a tragedy cannot be disputed.

Charles Ayer's theory of two heroines in
Corneille's tragedies seems highly useful when applied
to the fate of the heroines in the dénouements of all
the plays studied here.[278] Although Ayer's theory was
proffered to display how Corneille could assure the
presence of the love element in his tragedies, the
two-heroine theory does have strong repercussions for
the heroine at the end of the play. Corneille usually
offers two views on womanhood through the main
protagonist and a minor female character. In <u>Cinna</u>,
Emilie, the chief rebel in the play, represents a
"femme forte" whose rebellious and heroic behavior
found great favor with Corneille's public and: "has
been supposed to be drawn in accordance with the
nature of certain politically-minded women of

163

Corneille's times."[279] Livie is evidently more of an
example of a good or loving wife, who is more socially
acceptable than Emilie. Corneille offers two types,
or two views on women in order to satisfy all of his
spectators; however, the more socially acceptable
heroine, i.e., Livie, or Sabine and L'Infante, in the
earlier plays, receives the stamp of approval of the
patriarchal ruler or representative at the end of each
play. Corneille suggests the diversity of womankind
in his time by including two heroines in his
tragedies, but, his dénouements show how his
rebellious heroine's anger is crushed or abated by the
patriarchy, and how the more socially acceptable
heroine will be approved by conforming to patriarchal
expectations of her. Although Corneille's inclusion
and representation of strong images of women is highly
admirable, he in no way intends to upset the status
quo of his time, which he represents in his plays as a
world where heroines are forced to compromise their
desire for a more humane world, a world in which male
and female are equal, and not involved in a
destructive power struggle.

        Pauline's fate at the dénouement of the play is a
direct result of her father's political opportunism.
Not only does she have a husband and a lover because
of her father's errors, but she will suffer the loss
of Polyeucte's love, despite all the sacrifices she
had made on his behalf.

        Polyeucte claims he still loves her: "Je vous
aime, / Beaucoup moins que mon Dieu, mais bien plus
que moi-même" (Acte IV, Scène ii, 1279-80).   Yet,
Pauline is unable to understand a love that is so
abstract: "Tu préfères la mort à l'amour de Pauline!"
(Acte IV, Scène iii, 1287).   Furthermore, it
contradicts the reality of his actions that indicate a
desire for separation from her. Polyeucte is also out
of touch with Pauline's feelings when he subjects her
to an exchange in which Pauline is equated with
property. Polyeucte intends Pauline for Sévère after
his death:

                Possesseur d'un trésor dont je n'étois
                pas digne,
                Souffrez avant ma mort que je vous le
                résigne,
                . . . .
                Vous êtes digne d'elle, elle est digne
                de vous;

        Ne la refusez pas de la main d'un
        époux.
                (Acte IV, Scène iv, 1299-1300;
        1305-6)

However, Pauline does not take this matchmaking
lightly.

        Pauline angrily confronts her father, the less
then competent shaper of her fate, and Polyeucte, the
man she has sacrificed so much for:

        Qui   de   vous   deux   aujourd'hui
        m'assassine?
        Sont-ce tous deux ensemble, ou chacun à
        son tour?
        Ne pourrai-je fléchir la nature ou
        l'amour?
        Et n'obtiendrai-je rien d'un époux ni
        d'un père?
                (Acte V, Scène iii, 1580-83)

These are the two people, in Tastevin's estimation,
who should love her the most: "Pauline, palpitante
d'angoisse, implore à nouveau son père et son mari,
les deux êtres qui devraient la chérir, la protéger
contre la douleur et qui sont ses bourreaux."[280]
Pauline is being tortured instead of nurtured by the
two men in her life. As in the dénouements of the
three other plays in this study, harm will be done to
the heroine. Mauron most succinctly summarizes this
pattern in Corneille's dénouements: "Cependant, une
dissymétrie essentielle veut que le héros soit
invulnérable et l'héroïne blessée."[281]

        When Polyeucte repeats his desire to match Sévère
with Pauline ("Vivez avec Sévère," Acte V, Scène iii,
1584), he is cruelly separating himself from her.
Pauline continues to release her anger, which has
built up:

        Que t'ai-je fait, cruel, pour être
        ainsi traitée,
        Et pour me reprocher, au mépris de ma
        foi,
        Un amour si puissant que j'ai vaincu
        pour toi?
                (Acte V, Scène iii, 1592-94)

Her question is legitimate and reasonable. Why is she
being treated this way? Are there no rewards for her?

Why does Polyeucte not make an effort to be worthy of her: "Fais quelque effort sur toi pour te rendre à Pauline" (Acte V, Scène iii, 1600). Polyeucte remains very rigid in his determination to die, ignoring Pauline's words, and giving her two impossible alternatives: "Vivez avec Sévère, ou mourez avec moi" (Acte V, Scène iii, 1609). These are not real alternatives for Pauline and according to Allentuch no alternatives are available to her.[282] Polyeucte's rejection of Pauline is total, "Je ne vous connois plus, si vous n'êtes chrétienne" (Acte V, Scène iii, 1612).

Pauline's anger is centered on Félix, next. She tells him to take one last look at her: "Jetez sur votre fille un regard paternel: / Ma mort suivra la mort de ce cher criminel" (Acte V, Scène iii, 1621-22), before she too will die. She blames Félix because he is responsible for their marriage:

> Nos destins, par vos mains rendus inséparables,
> Nous doivent rendre heureux ensemble, ou misérables;
> Et vous seriez cruel jusques au dernier point,
> Si vous désunissiez ce que vous avez joint.
> (Acte V, Scène iii, 1627-30)

She also allies herself with Polyeucte in her effort to rebel against Félix. Polyeucte is, after all, her husband, and if he dies she should too: "Je te suivrai partout, et mourrai si tu meurs" (Acte V, Scène iii, 1681). Pauline then leaves with Polyeucte and witnesses his execution. Ayer stresses the importance and frequency of this technique in Corneille's dramaturgy, "Notice by the way that to die in the presence of the beloved one was, also a favorite idea of the heroes of Corneille."[283]

After Polyeucte's death, which Pauline has witnessed, she releases all of her anger at her father, who is responsible for all the hardship she has suffered:

> Père barbare, achève, achève ton ouvrage:
> . . . .
> Joins ta fille à ton gendre; ose: que tardes-tu?
> . . . .

Mon époux en mourant m'a laissé ses
lumières;
Son sang, dont tes bourreaux viennent
de me couvrir.
(Acte V, Scène v, 1719; 1721;
1724-25)

The sight of Polyeucte's death has liberated Pauline
from her father's authority:

Pauline's conversion, at the closing,
so long accepted solely as a work of
grace, humanly inexplicable, is speeded
perhaps by a quite unmiraculous
illumination: she learns from her
martyred husband how to untie the knot
of inner conflict and to turn hatred
outward.[284]

With this fact in mind, her conversion can be
understood in human terms.

Much controversy has surrounded Pauline's
conversion. Corneille actually prepared the
possibility of her conversion through Polyeucte, when
he says: "C'est en vain qu'on se met en défense: / Ce
Dieu touche les coeurs lorsque moins on y pense" (Acte
IV, Scène iii, 1275-76). Lancaster believes that not
only the shedding of Polyeucte's blood brings about
her conversion: ". . . but her devotion to him brings
about her conversion."[285] Abraham emphasizes the
shift in interpretation that has taken place from one
century to the next: "Her conversion, until the
nineteenth century, was most frequently seen as an act
of love rather than as the mystical experience that it
is considered today."[286] Nadal sees Pauline's
conversion as a gradual process brought about through
love:

Cet arrachement de Pauline à son milieu
ne se fait pas d'un coup, . . . ni
seulement par le baptême du sang du
martyr sur la face de sa femme, mais
aussi et plus lentement par les voies
de l'amour humain.[287]

Sweetser gives her own interpretation of the
conversion, and summarizes all the controversy
surrounding it:

> Corneille suggère une évolution des
> sentiments de l'héroïne, désirant sans
> doute rendre sa conversion plausible.
> Le seul effet de la grâce pouvait gêner
> un public formé dans une tradition
> humaniste et touché par la pensée
> rationaliste. Il convenait sans doute
> d'y ajouter des justifications reposant
> sur la psychologie attribuée au
> personnage. Le double aspect de la
> conversion de Pauline, divin et humain,
> se traduit par une diversité
> d'interprétation de la part de la
> critique, les uns soutenant la primauté
> de la grâce, les autres celle des
> acheminements humains.[288]

Sweetser indicates that two distinct camps of criticism coexist concerning Pauline's conversion. The less convincing interpretation, after the close attention given to Pauline's role in this study, is the divine interpretation, which Abraham emphasizes is the most popular today.[289] The reason for the lack of confidence we have in the divine interpretation as it affects Pauline, is that it contradicts all that we have learned about her role and the reaction of Corneille's contemporaries to it. The fact that the Hotel de Rambouillet did not approve of the sacred theme in Polyeucte can also be taken as an indication of the dramatic and aesthetic tastes of the French, as dictated by this powerful salon. Corneille himself, because of the disapproval of the Hotel de Rambouillet, learned that the religious theme of the play would not be favored by his public, but rather, as Descotes has discovered, that the love interest surrounding Pauline and Sévère would win the approval of his audience.

In light of this evidence, it seems that the human interpretation of Pauline's conversion is plausible. The divine interpretation obscures the reality of Pauline's anger against her father, which is an important element of her character in the play. Also, the divine intervention is used as a closure device, i.e., to bring about the dénouement, but it is not convincing when we examine Pauline's psychological evolution.[290] Allentuch is not inaccurate when she describes the religious theme as adornment, especially as it affects Pauline's role.

It is possible to view Pauline's conversion not only in divine terms but also to examine her conversion as it affects her characterization, in human terms. By paying close attention to Pauline's characterization, we can interpret her conversion as another way in which she arms herself against her father's cruelty, and uses Polyeucte's martyrdom as an example of supremely rebellious behavior, which she can emulate to break all the chains[291] of her tie to her father's and all earthly authority.

NOTES

249. "In all events, the long-standing criticism that
     Corneille's portrayal of women lacks poetic
     truth, when compared with his portrayal of men,
     turns out to be in error. Corneille endows his
     heroines with more capacity for protest and more
     aggression than some of his critics could allow."
     See Harriet Allentuch, "Reflections on Women in
     the Theater of Corneille," Kentucky Romance
     Quarterly, Vol. XXI, No. 1 (1974), p. 111.

250. Maria Tastevin, Les Héroïnes de Corneille, p. 19.

251. Tastevin, p. 27.

252. See Ian MacLean, Woman Triumphant . . . , p. 11;
     p. 55. Women were traditionally thought to have
     greater powers of memory and imagination than men
     well into the 17th century. This was attributed
     to the predominance of moist humours in their
     blood.

253. This phenomenon also occurred in Le Cid and
     Horace and is pointed out by Tastevin with regard
     to Cinna. See Les Héroïnes de Corneille, pp.
     79-80.

254. Tastevin, p. 16.

255. Tastevin, pp. 18-19.

256. Robert J. Nelson, Corneille, His Heroes and Their
     Worlds (Philadelphia: University of Pennsylvania
     Press, 1963), p. 76.

257. See Claude Vigée's article, "La Princesse de
     Clèves et la Tradition du Refus," in Critique
     (août-septembre, 1960), pp. 723-54, for an
     interesting discussion of the theme of retreat
     from the world present in La Princesse de Clèves
     and in other 17th century texts. Chimène's
     desires to retreat from the world at the
     dénouement of Le Cid may be linked to this
     tradition.

258. Serge Doubrovsky, Corneille et la dialectique du
     héros, p. 165. (Doubrovsky goes as far as to say
     that Camille's death is the crowning of the play.
     P. 156.)

259. Claude Abraham, Pierre Corneille, pp. 62-3.

260. L'Abbé d'Aubignac, La Pratique du Théâtre, p.
___.

261. Henry Carrington Lancaster, A History of French
Dramatic Literature . . . , Part II, Vol. I, pp.
303-4.

262. Maria Tastevin, Les Héroïnes de Corneille, pp.
66-7.

263. Eva Figes, Tragedy and Social Evolution, p. 127.

264. Marie-Odile Sweetser, La Dramaturgie de
Corneille. (Paris: Droz, 1977), p. 117.

265. Catharine Stimpson, "Sex, Gender, and American
Culture," in Women and Men: Changing Roles,
Relationships . . . eds. Libby A. Cater and Anne
Firor Scott (New York: Praeger, 1977), p. 225.

266. Harriet R. Allentuch, "Reflections on Women in
the Theater of Corneille," p. 97.

267. Allentuch, p. 109.

268. See footnote #115.

269. Gustave Lanson, Corneille (Paris: Hachette,
1800), p. 108.

270. André Stegmann, L'Héroïsme Cornélien, Vol. II
(Paris: Armand Colin, 1968), p. 587.

271. Serge Doubrovsky, Corneille et la dialectique du
héros, p. 216.

272. Roger Zuber, "La Conversion d'Emilie," Héroïsme
et Création Littéraire Sous Les Règnes D'Henri IV
et De Louis XIII, eds. Noémi Hepp et Georges
Livet (Paris: Klincksieck, 1974), p. 276.

273. Marie-Odile Sweetser, La Dramaturgie de
Corneille, p. 121.

274. Maria Tastevin, Les Héroïnes de Corneille, p. 90.

275. Harriet Ray Allentuch, "The Problem of Cinna,"
The French Review, vol. XLVIII, No. 5 (April,
1975), p. 885. A recent article on Emilie does

very little in the way of rehabilitating her character. The authors insist that Emilie recognizes Auguste as her "conqueror" and submits to him. See "Cinna ou L'Agenouillement d'Emilie devant la Clémence d'Auguste" by Wolfgang Leiner and Sheila Bayne in Onze Etudes sur l'image de la femme dans la littérature française du dix-septième siècle, ed. Wolfgang Leiner (Paris: Jean-Michel Place, 1978), p. 206.

276. Maria Tastevin, Les Héroïnes de Corneille, p. 85.

277. Henry Carrington Lancaster, A History of French Dramatic Literature in the Seventeenth Century, Part II, Vol. I (Baltimore: Johns Hopkins, 1932), p. 317.

278. Charles Ayer, The Tragic Heroines of Corneille, p. 27.

279. Lancaster, p. 316.

280. Tastevin, p. 128.

281. Charles Mauron, Des Métaphores Obsédantes au Mythe Personnel, p. 254.

282. Harriet R. Allentuch, "Pauline and the Princesse de Clèves," MLQ, p. 182.

283. Charles C. Ayer, The Tragic Heroines of Pierre Corneille, p. 68.

284. Allentuch, p. 178.

285. Henry Carrington Lancaster, A History of French Dramatic Literature in the Seventeenth Century, Part II, Vol. I, p. 325.

286. Claude Abraham, Pierre Corneille, p. 74.

287. Octave Nadal, Le sentiment de l'amour dans l'oeuvre de Pierre Corneille, p. 205.

288. Marie-Odile Sweetser, La Dramaturgie de Corneille. (Genève-Paris: Droz, 1977), p. 124.

289. See Claude Abraham, Pierre Corneille. (New York: Twayne, 1978), p. 74.

290. Allentuch gives strong arguments for the human interpretation of Pauline's conversion. See her article: "Pauline and the Princesse de Clèves," MLQ, p. 178.

291. Allentuch, p. 178.

CONCLUSION

In the preceding chapters of this study, I have
focused my attention on five Cornelian tragic
heroines. I have treated these heroines as a group
that is separate from the heroes. I have done this
for three reasons. First, in an effort to correct
what I have detected as a male bias in criticism
against the heroines. Second, I have attempted to
demonstrate the importance of the heroines in their
own right. Shulamith Firestone explains why it is
important to study "female reality" in literature: ".
. . an exploration of the strictly female reality is a
necessary step to correct the warp in a sexually
biased culture."[292] Third, I have tried to discover
the heroines' ethic, as created by a male author, and
the values they defend or espouse.

Through a close textual reading and study of the
female protagonists in Le Cid, Horace, Cinna, and
Polyeucte, I have attempted to restore the heroines to
their dramatic contexts and to see them as characters
in plays. I have scrutinized the heroines' words and
their actions in order to measure how well they
correspond to each other. I have also examined the
heroines in the light of their socio-political status
as representations of women in the seventeenth century
in France. Despite the limitations placed on women at
this time, I have shown how the heroines were depicted
as able to master their destinies and be
self-determining. I have directed my attention to the
best known of Corneille's heroines and have found that
there is still much more to be said about them.

Before a determination can be made concerning
Corneille's tragic heroines as authentic "images of
women," it is necessary to mention several factors
that will make this possible. The importance of women
and their influence on Corneille's theater has been
recognized by Ayer, Lathuillère, and MacLean. Through
their efforts it is now possible to prove that
Corneille wrote for an audience in which women played
a significant role. In fact, the women in Corneille's
audience influenced the types of heroines he presented
on the stage:

> A l'époque du Cid, d'Horace, et de
> Polyeucte, la réhabilitation humaniste
> et chrétienne de la femme contribue
> puissamment à la formation d'un public

féminin, prêt à applaudir Sabine et Pauline.[293]

Stemann stresses the humanist and Christian "apologie de la femme" that was taking place in France during Corneille's dramatic career. He also acknowledges the existence of a female public to whose tastes Corneille catered. MacLean completes the picture by stating that through the influence of women, the presence of heroic women in imaginative literature, was an achievement of the period in which Corneille wrote. He also states that feminism had an influence on the drama of this period: ". . . there are also parallels to be drawn between the subject-matter of drama and of feminist literature of this period."[294] Lathuillère emphasizes that an apology of women took place in Corneille's theater which the "précieuses" admired:

> Les précieuses, et avec elles nombre de critiques contemporains, unissent dans une égale admiration l'auteur de Clélie et celui d'Oedipe. A leurs yeux, l'un et l'autre ont fait avec autant de bonheur l'apologie de la femme et de l'amour. . . .[295]

He also indicates that Corneille was aware of this literary movement and its admiration for his tragic heroines.[296]

As we have seen, a significant example of the influence of women on Corneille's theater is the presence and weighting of the love element in his tragedies. It is possible to trace a progression in this theme's development from Le Cid to Polyeucte. In Le Cid and Horace, the love element is given equal treatment with the political element. A change begins to occur in Cinna where love becomes thematically inseparable from the conspiracy, the political element. In Polyeucte, the fusion of these two themes is complete. The marriage of Pauline is the source from which the political element is derived. In fact, the political aspect of this tragedy is less developed and less important. As a result of the shift of emphasis from politics to the love element, Polyeucte focuses with more depth on the psychology of Pauline. One final dimension of the influence of women which brought about the increasing presence of love in tragedy, is that love is the foundation of the female ethic. As love equals and rivals politics as a tragic

theme, the female ethic also provides an alternative
to male heroics.

Another factor that is important to our
understanding of Corneille's heroines is Ayer's
two-heroine theory. Ayer formulated a theory based on
Corneille's use of two heroines in his tragic theater.
He showed how Corneille introduced the love element
and assured its presence in his tragedies through the
repetition of the use of two heroines.[297] According
to this theory, a female protagonist such as Chimène,
is complemented by a secondary female character such
as L'Infante, whose function is to introduce the love
element in Le Cid. This theory also applies to
Horace, where Sabine introduces the love theme;
however, her role is much more important than
L'Infante's. In the case of Cinna and Polyeucte, I
have had to interpret Ayer's two-heroine theory
differently. In Cinna, Emilie reveals her love for
Cinna and another heroine is not necessary for that
function; however, Livie is contrasted with Emilie.
In effect, she presents another type of woman. Livie
is the heroine who conforms to the dictates of
patriarchal society. She not only assists her
husband, Auguste, in his political role as emperor:
she is the one who suggests clemency for the
conspirators; but she also represents a female who is
socially acceptable in her behavior. In Polyeucte,
Pauline also introduces the love element; yet, the
major difference between this play and the three
others studied is that Pauline is the sole heroine.
An evolution has occurred in Corneille's female
characterization. In Cinna and Polyeucte, Corneille
was able to assure the presence of love without the
second heroine; however, the difference between these
two tragedies is that Pauline is the only heroine
present in the entire play. The absence of a second
heroine attests to the fact that Corneille's female
characterization developed. He was able to create a
heroine who introduced her own love without the use of
a second heroine. Another important facet of a
two-heroine theory is that the presence of two
heroines not only gives Corneille's audience two types
of women, but also two female alternatives to
contemplate and emulate.

The final consideration, in a feminist approach
to Corneille's heroines, is the issue of authenticity.
Are his heroines authentic as "images of women"? How
can we determine his perspective on them? First, it
is necessary to define the meaning of authenticity in

a feminist interpretation of the "image of women" in the work of a male author. Josephine Donovan gives us such a definition:

> . . . one of the primary criteria by which feminist critics are judging works of literature is by what one might call the "truth criterion." . . . That is, we are making judgements based on an assessment of the authenticity of women characters, women's situations, and the author's perspective on them. . . .
>
> The feminist critic maintains, in short, that there are truths and probabilities about the female experience that form a criterion against which to judge the authenticity of a literary statement about women.[298]

Since Corneille is a dramatist, it is necessary to examine the fate of his heroines at the dénouement in order to determine their authenticity. A careful look at the dénouements of the four plays in question will also help us gauge Corneille's perspective on his heroines.

Let us now look at the fate of Chimène, Sabine, Camille, Emilie, and Pauline at the dénouements of all four plays. Although Chimène refuses to be silenced and resists male authority throughout the play, the king orders her to be Rodrigue's wife in a year's time. The dénouement of Le Cid is known for its open-endedness; however, as far as Chimène's fate is concerned there is little ambiguity. Chimène's only desire at the dénouement is to renounce this world and retreat to a convent. Chimène's double fate, or seemingly double fate--she is actually being ordered to marry Rodrigue--is Corneille's choice. Like Chimène, Sabine is silenced at the dénouement. She is forced to accept values that are alien to her: she is married to a murderer, in fact, he is her brothers' murderer. Camille's fate is much more brutal. She is murdered by her brother, and as Catharine Stimpson points out, as a tragic heroine she falls alone.[299] Camille perishes because she is a threat to a patriarchal world represented by Horace. Camille refuses to accept values that violate her ethic and she is destroyed as a result. The dénouement of Horace is also considered open-ended because the issues involved, especially Camille's murder, are never resolved. This is particularly troubling for a determination of Corneille's perspective on Camille. Emilie is an interesting heroine who is as adamant as Camille about her values, and who, unlike Camille, survives at the dénouement. Emilie has some bargaining power, so to speak, as far as her fate is concerned. She accepts Auguste's clemency after she believes that she has satisfied her right to vengeance. However, Emilie's isolation at the dénouement indicates that her rebelliousness is not acceptable in the patriarchal world she inhabits. While Emilie was aware of her ability to be involved in political activity, Pauline is aware of her political importance. Pauline's conversion, at the dénouement, is part of her rebellion against her father. Her conversion is a result of the fact that she witnessed Polyeucte's death and was inspired by his rebellious behavior. She is the only heroine in this study who truly liberates herself from patriarchal oppression at the dénouement of the play. There is no further authority that can dominate her.

Although the pattern in the four dénouements we have just examined is one of increasing degrees of strength in the heroines, Corneille's perspective on them seems to match that of the patriarchal "ordre du monde" that dominates his tragedies. Chimène will be forced to marry Rodrigue; Sabine is silenced and forced to accept a husband who has murdered his sister and her brothers; Camille is murdered in cold blood; Emilie is forced to abandon her right to vengeance against an illegitimate king, and she is silenced by another woman, Livie; finally Pauline will be rejected by all those who are supposed to love her. Corneille's representation of strong women ("femmes fortes") reflects the on-going "apologie de la femme" which occurred in the seventeenth century, and is probably due to the tastes of his female public; however, he does not attempt to violate the structure and demands of patriarchal society. He in no way tries to upset the status quo of the society represented in his tragedies. Corneille's heroines are repeatedly forced to compromise their desire for a more humane world. His dénouements indicate how rebellion or anger in the heroines is crushed, and how more socially acceptable behavior will be approved of by patriarchal expectations of them. As a result, his heroines are authentic as women who reflect female experience under a patriarchy. They are true to life as women who manifest their strength and determine their fate, in any way that is possible to them, despite their forced oppression and limited political power in a patriarchal world.

292. Shulamith Firestone, _The Dialectic of Sex_ (New York: Bantam Books, 1971), p. 167.

293. André Stegmann, _L'Héroïsme Cornélien_, Vol. II (Paris: Armand Colin, 1968), p. 270.

294. Ian MacLean, _Woman Triumphant: Feminism in French Literature, 1610-1652_ (Oxford: Oxford University Press, 1977), pp. 269; 179.

295. Roger Lathuillère, _La Préciosité: Etude historique et linguistique_. Vol. I (Genève: Droz, 1966), p. 467.

296. Lathuillère, pp. 459; 467.

297. Charles C. Ayer, _The Tragic Heroines of Pierre Corneille_ ((Strassburg: Heitz, 1898), p. 28.

298. Josephine Donovan, "Afterword: Critical Re-Vision" in _Feminist Literary Criticism_, ed. Josephine Donovan (Lexington: University Press of Kentucky, 1975), p. 77.

299. Catharine Stimpson, "Sex, Gender, and American Culture," in _Women and Men: Changing Roles, Relationships and Perceptions_, eds. Libby A. Cater and Anne Firor Scott (New York: Praeger, 1977), p. 225.

BIBLIOGRAPHY

Primary Sources

Aubignac, François Hédelin, Abbé D'. La Pratique du
Théâtre. Ed. Pierre Martino. 1657; rpt. Paris:
Honoré Champion, 1927.

Balzac, Jean Louis Guez, Sieur de. Lettres Choisies
Du Sr De Balzac. Leiden: les Elseviers, 1652.

Chapelain, Jean. Les Sentimens de L'Académie
Françoise sur la Tragi-Comédie Du Cid. Ed.
Georges Collas. 1637; rpt. Genève: Slatkine
Reprints, 1968.

Corneille, Pierre. Le Cid. Ed. Maurice Cauchie.
1637; rpt. Paris: Marcel Didier, 1946.

_____. Oeuvres de Pierre Corneille. Ed. Charles
Marty-Laveaux. Paris: Librairie de L. Hachette,
1862. Vols. I and III.

Le Dictionnaire de l'Académie françoise. Paris:
Académie françoise, 1694.

Furetière, Antoine. Dictionnaire universel. Paris:
1690.

Scudéry, Georges de. Observations sur le Cid. Ed.
Armand Gasté. 1637; rpt. Genève: Slatkine
Reprints, 1970.

Secondary Sources

Abraham, Claude. Pierre Corneille. New York: Twayne
Publishers, 1972.

Adam, Antoine. Histoire de la Littérature Française
au XVIIe Siècle. Paris: Editions Mondiales,
1962. Vol. I.

_____. Le Théâtre Classique. Paris: Presses
Universitaires de France, 1970.

Albistur, Maïté, and Daniel Armogathe. Histoire de
Féminisme Français: du moyen âge à nos jours.
Paris: Editions des Femmes, 1977.

Allentuch, Harriet R. "Pauline and the Princesse de Clèves." Modern Language Quarterly, Vol. XXX, No. 2 (June, 1969), pp. 171-82.

_____. "The Problem of Cinna." The French Review, Vol. XLVIII, No. 5 (April, 1975), pp. 878-86.

_____. "Reflections on Women in the Theater of Corneille." Kentucky Romance Quarterly, Vol. XXI, No. 1 (1974), pp. 97-111.

Ayer, Charles Carlton. The Tragic Heroines of Pierre Corneille. Strassburg: J. H. ED. Heitz, 1898.

Backer, Dorothy Anne Liot. Precious Women. New York: Basic Books, 1974.

Bénichou, Paul. Morales du Grand Siècle. Paris: Gallimard, 1948.

Borgerhoff, E. B. O. The Freedom of French Classicism. Princeton: Princeton University Press, 1950.

Bray, René. La Formation de la Doctrine Classique. Paris: Nizet, 1951.

Brunetière, Ferdinand. Etudes Critiques sur L'Histoire de la Littérature Française. Paris: Librairie Hachette, 1911. Vol. VI.

_____. Histoire de la Littérature Française Classique, 1515-1830. Paris: Librairie Ch. Delagrave, 1904. Vol. II.

_____. "L'Influence des Femmes." In Questions de Critique. Paris: Calmann-Levy, 1888, pp. 23-61.

Cater, Libby A., and Anne Firor Scott. Women and Men: Changing Roles, Relationships and Perceptions. New York: Praeger, 1977.

Cayrou, Gaston. Le Français Classique: Lexique de la Langue du Dix-Septième Siècle. Paris: Didier, 1948.

Cloonan, William. "Women in Horace." Romance Notes, Vol. XVI, No. 3 (Spring, 1975), pp. 647-52.

Collins, Marie, and Sylvie Weil Sayre, eds. <u>Les</u> <u>Femmes en France</u>. New York: Charles Scribner's Sons, 1974.

Couton, Georges. <u>Corneille</u>. Paris: Hatier, 1958.

_____. "Etat présent des études cornéliennes." <u>Information Littéraire</u>, 8 (1956), pp. 43-48.

_____. <u>Réalisme de Corneille</u>: <u>La Clef de Mélite</u>; <u>Réalitiés dans Le Cid</u>. Paris: Société d'Edition "Les Belles Lettres," 1953.

Davidson, Hugh M. <u>Audience, Words, and Art</u>: <u>Studies in Seventeenth-Century French Rhetoric</u>. Columbus: Ohio State University Press, 1965.

Decaux, Alain. <u>Histoire des Françaises</u>. 2 vols. Paris: Librairie Académique Perrin, 1972.

Descotes, Maurice. <u>Les Grands Rôles du Théâtre de Corneille</u>. Paris: Presses Universitaires de France, 1962.

Donovan, Josephine. "Afterword: Critical Re-vision." In <u>Feminist Literary Criticism</u>. Ed. Josephine Donovan. Lexington: University Press of Kentucky, 1975, pp. 74-81.

_____. <u>Feminist Literary Criticism</u>. Lexington: University Press of Kentucky, 1975.

Dort, Bernard. <u>Corneille: dramaturge</u>. Paris: L'Arche, 1957.

Doubrovsky, Serge. <u>Corneille: et la dialectique du héros</u>. Paris: Gallimard, 1963.

Droz, E. "Corneille et L'Astrée." <u>Revue d'Histoire littéraire</u>, 28 (1921), pp. 161-203; 361-87.

Dubois, Elfrieda T. "The Education of Women in Seventeenth-Century France." <u>French Studies</u>, Vol. XXXII, No. 1 (January, 1978), pp. 1-19.

Duchene, Roger. "L'Ecole des Femmes au XVIIe Siècle." In <u>Mélanges offerts à Georges Mongrédien</u>, No. II (1974). Limoges: Société d'Etudes du XVIIe Siècle, pp. 143-172.

Edelman, Nathan, ed. "The Seventeenth Century." In A
Critical Bibliography of French Literature. Gen.
eds. David C. Cabeen and Jules Brody. Syracuse:
Syracuse University Press, 1961. Vol. III.

Faguet, Emile. En Lisant Corneille. Paris:
Hachette, 1913.

_____. Dix-Septième Siècle: Etudes Littéraires.
Paris: Boivin, 1887.

Figes, Eva. Tragedy and Social Evolution. London:
John Calder, 1976.

Firestone, Shulamith. The Dialectic of Sex. New
York: Bantam Books, 1971.

Fogel, Herbert. The Criticism of Cornelian Tragedy.
New York: Exposition Press, 1967.

Gasté, Armand, ed. La Querelle du Cid: Pièces et
Pamphlets. Genève: Slatkine Reprints, 1970.

Goode, William O. "Hand, Heart, and Mind: The
Complexity of the Heroic Quest in Le Cid." PMLA,
Vol. 91, No. 1 (January, 1976), pp. 44-53.

Guiraud, Pierre. Index du Vocabulaire du Théâtre
Classique: Corneille I: Index des Mots de
Cinna; Corneille II: Index des Mots du Cid;
Corneille III: Index des Mots d'Horace;
Corneille IV: Index des Mots de Polyeucte.
Paris: Klincksieck, 1955, 1955, 1956, 1957.

Heilbrun, Carolyn, and Catharine Stimpson. "Theories
of Feminist Criticism: A Dialogue." In Feminist
Literary Criticism. Ed. Josephine Donovan.
Lexington: University Press of Kentucky, 1975,
pp. 61-73.

Hepp, Noëmi, and Georges Livet. Héroïsme et Création
Littéraire Sous Les Règnes d'Henri IV et de Louis
XIII. Actes et Colloques No. 16. Paris:
Editions Klincksieck, 1974.

Herland, Louis. Corneille par lui-même. Paris:
Seuil, 1954.

_____. Horace, ou la naissance de l'homme. Paris:
Editions de Minuit, 1952.

Holly, Marcia. "Consciousness and Authenticity: Toward a Feminist Aesthetic." In Feminist Literary Criticism. Ed. Josephine Donovan. Lexington: University Press of Kentucky, 1975, pp. 38-47.

Kelly-Gadol, Joan. "The Social Relation of the Sexes: Methodological Implications of Women's History." Signs, Vol. 1, No. 4 (Summer, 1976), pp. 809-23.

Krailsheimer, A. J. Studies in Self-Interest: from Descartes to La Bruyère. Oxford: Clarendon Press, 1962.

Lancaster, Henry Carrington. The French Tragi-Comedy: Its Origin and Development from 1552 to 1628. Baltimore: J. H. Furst, 1907.

_____. A History of French Dramatic Literature in the Seventeenth Century. Baltimore: The Johns Hopkins Press, 1929. Vol. II, Part I.

_____. A History of French Dramatic Literature in the Seventeenth Century. Baltimore: The Johns Hopkins Press, 1932. Vol. I, Part II.

Lanson, Gustave. Corneille. Paris: Librairie Hachette, 1898.

_____. Esquisse D'Une Histoire de la Tragédie Française. Paris: Honoré Champion, 1954.

_____. "Le Héros et le généreux selon Descartes." Revue d'Histoire littéraire de la France, Vol. I (1894), pp. 397-411.

Lathuillère, Roger. La Préciosité: Etude historique et linguistique. Genève: Droz, 1966. Vol. I.

LeGuiner, Jeanne. Les Femmes dans Les Tragédies de Corneille. Quimper: Imprimerie Vre Ed. Menez, 1920.

Leiner, Wolfgang, and Sheila Bayne. "Cinna ou L'Agenouillement D'Emilie Devant La Clémence D'Auguste." In Onze Etudes sur l'image de la femme dans la littérature française du dix-septième siècle. Ed. Wolfgang Leiner. Paris: Jean-Michel Place, 1978, pp. 195-219.

Lougee, Carolyn C. Le Paradis des femmes: Women, Salons and Social Stratification in 17th-century France. Princeton: Princeton University Press, 1976.

Lough, John. Paris Theatre Audiences in the Seventeenth and Eighteenth Centuries. London: Oxford University Press, 1957.

MacLean, Ian. Woman Triumphant: Feminism in French Literature, 1610-1652. Oxford: Oxford University Press, 1977.

Margitić, Milorad R. "Corneille, Un Humaniste Intégral." Papers on French Seventeenth Century Literature, No. 8 (Winter 1977-78), pp. 135-56.

Maurens, Jacques. La Tragédie sans Tragique. Paris: Armand Colin, 1966.

Mauron, Charles. Des Métaphores Obsédantes au Mythe Personnel. Paris: Librairie Jose Corti, 1964.

May, Georges. "Sept années d'études cornéliennes." Romanic Review, Vol. XLIII, No. 4 (December, 1952, pp. 282-92.

_____. Tragédie Cornélienne, Tragédie Racinienne. Urbana: University of Illinois Press, 1948.

Miller, Jean Baker. Toward a New Psychology of Women. Boston: Beacon Press, 1976.

Moore, Will G. "Corneille's 'Horace' and the Interpretation of French Classical Drama." Modern Language Review, Vol. XXXIV (1939), pp. 382-95.

Muratore, Mary Jo. The Evolution of the Cornelian Heroine. Potomac, Maryland: Studia Humanitatis, 1982.

Nadal, Octave. Le Sentiment de l'amour dans l'oeuvre de Pierre Corneille. Paris: Gallimard, 1948.

Nelson, Robert J. Corneille, His Heroes and Their Worlds. Philadelphia: University of Pennsylvania Press, 1963.

Péguy, Charles. Oeuvres En Prose, 1909-1914. Ed. Marcel Péguy. Paris: Gallimard, 1961. vol. II.

_____. Victor-Marie, comte Hugo. Paris: Gallimard, 1935.

Pratt, Annis V. "The New Feminist Criticisms: Exploring the History of the New Space." In Beyond Intellectual Sexism: A New Woman, A New Reality. New York: David McKay Company, 1976, pp. 175-95.

Register, Cheri. "American Feminist Literary Criticism: A Bibliographical Introduction." In Feminist Literary Criticism. Ed. Josephine Donovan. Lexington: University Press of Kentucky, 1975, pp. 1-28.

Rubin, Elaine R. "The Heroic Image: Women and Power in Early-Seventeenth Century France, 1610-1661." Dissertation: George Washington University, 1977.

Scherer, Jacques. La Dramaturgie Classique en France. Paris: Librairie Nizet, 1950.

Schlumberger, Jean. Plaisir à Corneille. Paris: Gallimard, 1936.

Sellstrom, A. Donald. "The Structure of Corneille's Masterpeices." Romanic Review, Vol. XLIX (1958), pp. 269-77.

Smith-Rosenberg, Carroll. "The New Woman and the New History." Feminist Studies, Vol. 3, No. 1-2 (Fall, 1975), pp. 189-96.

Stegmann, André. L'Héroïsme Cornélien: Genèse et Signification. Paris: Armand Colin, 1968. Vol. II.

Stimpson, Catharine R. "Sex, Gender, and American Culture." In Women and Men: Changing Roles, Relationships and Perceptions. New York: Praeger, 1977.

Sweetser, Marie-Odile. Les Conceptions Dramatiques de Corneille. Genève: Droz, 1962.

_____. La Dramaturgie de Corneille. Genève: Droz, 1977.

Tastevin, Maria. Les Héroïnes de Corneille. Paris: Edouard Champion, 1924.

189

Vigée, Claude. "La Princesse de Clèves et la tradition du refus." *Critique*, Vol. 159-60 (1960), pp. 723-54.

Voltaire. *Commentaires sur Corneille*. Paris: Firmin-Didot, 1800.

Wiley, W. L. *The Early Public Theatre in France*. Cambridge: Harvard University Press, 1960.

Yarrow, P. J. *Corneille*. London: MacMillan & Company, 1963.

Zuber, Roger. "La Conversion d'Emilie." In *Héroïsme et Création Littéraire Sous Les Règnes d'Henri IV et de Louis XIII*. Ed. Noémi Hepp and Georges Livet. Paris: Klincksieck, 1974, pp. 261-76.

APPENDIX

MARIA TASTEVIN MILLER:
FRENCH PRE-FEMINIST SCHOLAR

In 1980, when I completed my doctoral
dissertation, I believed that I had thoroughly
researched my feminist critical interpretation of
Pierre Corneille's tragic heroines. To refresh your
memories, Pierre Corneille was the seventeenth century
French dramatist who founded French tragedy and wrote
thirty-two plays. He is known primarily for creating
heroes who aspire to reach the heights of
self-actualization. Accordingly, the Cornelian
bibliography could be described as a canon on the hero
and male heroism.

The one exception to that canon was the 1924
book, Les Héroines De Corneille, written by Maria
Tastevin, a French professor at Vassar College from
1922-1954. This book, which was central to my
feminist critique of Corneille's heroines, was
virtually ignored in male scholarship in France and in
the United States. Only two bibliographies of French
literature, and two critical works on Corneille's
heroes, make mention of Maria Tastevin's book. This
neglect is odd especially in view of the fact that
Maria Tastevin was awarded on June 23, 1925, the
"palmes académiques" award giving her the title of
"Officer of Public Education." The French Academy, a
male bastion of literary recognition, which excluded
the writer, Colette, from its membership, presented
Maria Tastevin with a silver medal in recognition of
her book.

In my own research on Corneille's heroines, I
felt a deep debt to Maria Tastevin. She had applied a
method of literary criticism, which easily joined the
style of feminist literary criticism that I was
practicing in 1980. Tastevin courageously challenged
a vast body of male scholarship including that of
Voltaire, Lanson, and Sarcey, in order to negate a
trend in Cornelian criticism, predating 1924, which
reflected a harsh bias against the heroines. In the
preface of her book, Tastevin states that:

> Cornelian heroines have
> particularly suffered from preconceived
> ideas. Once in awhile, a voice is
> raised in her favor, but current
> opinion hardly seems modified. It is

191

common usage to state that they are too
virile, too grandiloquent, too proud,
in a word, that they are not real women
. . . I will not surprise my reader
when I say from this point on that my
conclusions do not conform to the
traditional views held on Corneille's
women.*

Tastevin mentioned two points that were crucial for my
feminist critique of Corneille's heroines. The first
is "preconceived ideas" or what I termed bias, and the
second is "traditional opinions of women" or what I
termed stereotypes. Tastevin, like feminist critics
after her, took the stance of defending Cornelian
heroines against male bias and male stereotypes of
women. With a sense of urgency, Tastevin presented a
perceptive psychological and moral "re-vision" of six
Cornelian heroines. She managed to explore their
motivations and psychology from a more authentic,
female standpoint and to prove that Cornelian heroines
were highly complex and well-developed characters in
their own right.

Maria Tastevin's emphasis on the need to
reinterpret Corneille's heroines is in harmony with
current modes of feminist literary criticism. Her
analysis entailed three stages. First, she identified
bias and stereotyping in male scholarship towards
Corneille's heroines; then, she negated them through a
detailed analysis of each heroine; and, finally she
defended the heroines by showing that their values
were different from or opposed to those of the heroes.
The nature of my own examination of Corneille's
heroines derives from the tradition begun by Tastevin.

I decided to examine Tastevin's life further and
work in an effort to restore her contribution to
feminist literary criticism and Cornelian criticism,
to make her available to a wider public, and to
present her life as a prototype of a courageous
pre-feminist woman scholar.

In 1982, I called the archives at Vassar College
and asked a librarian to locate the file of Maria
Tastevin. I was puzzled to hear that she could not
locate one. I was, however, referred to Anne
Gittlemann, Chair of the French Department at Vassar.
Anne Gittlemann gave me two critical pieces of
information. First, that Maria Tastevin had married
and that her married name was Miller and, second, that

she was still alive at 94 and living in Paris.

After my conversation with Anne Gittlemann, I
telephoned the same librarian in Vassar's archives. I
informed her of Maria Tastevin's married name and
asked her to locate the file. She searched for it and
still no file turned up. The librarian believed that
Maria Tastevin's husband, John Richardson Miller, had
also taught at Vassar. She looked under his name,
thumbed through his file, and located Maria Tastevin's
file. Her file had literally been stuffed into her
husband's file despite her 32 years of teaching
experience at Vassar. Tastevin's file was not
classified under either her single or married name.
The contents of the file were sent to me by the
librarian who assured me that she would create a
separate file for Tastevin Miller that same day.
Despite my shock that such a sexist filing system was
used at Vassar, I was relieved that my phone call
helped restore her file to its rightful place.

Shortly after I learned that Tastevin Miller was
still alive, I wrote her a long letter. I was curious
to learn how capable of corresponding and how lucid
she was. In my letter, I informed her that I would be
in Paris in March of 1983, and that I would like to
interview her at that time. I was delighted to
receive a speedy response in which she assured me that
she would love to meet me and grant me an interview.
What I intended to achieve through this interview was
to add a personal dimension in a real life meeting
with her, to gain insight into her life, and to return
her gift to me by celebrating and making public her
contribution to feminist scholarship.

The night of my arrival in Paris, I received a
phone message from Maria Tastevin Miller. I returned
the call and our first conversation was a delight! We
scheduled a three-hour interview one week in advance.

When I arrived at her apartment, I was greeted by
a thin, grey-haired woman, conservatively dressed, who
gave me a warm welcome and showed me into her living
room. After I sat down, Maria Tastevin Miller offered
me a shot of Samoze, a sweet Greek wine. Much to my
surprise, she then walked over to her fireplace where
she stored her bottle of Samoze behind a few logs. We
both drank our shot of Samoze before I began the
interview. I had all of my questions prepared in
advance, and as I loaded my tape recorder, she laughed
and said, "Mademoiselle Schmidt, you are so precise;

you Americans are so organized."

I was immediately impressed by Tastevin Miller's quickness of mind, memory, and professorial precision in prefatory statements, which were always followed by laughter. For example, she would say, "I don't want to tell you inaccurate things" or, "Please wait, I don't want to make any false statements." She would also remind me of her age and say, "My stories are almost prehistoric. Don't forget my age," and, "You know, the Eiffel Tower is my age." (Maria Tastevin was born in 1888 and the Eiffel Tower was opened by 1889.) I later learned that her memory was astonishingly accurate. In fact, she remembered where the reviews of her book were published, which was very helpful, since this information was not in her file.

My first question was why she chose Corneille's heroines as a topic for her book. She said, "The heroines interested me a great deal because they showed their will. I would read critics who didn't think at all as I did about the heroines, and I found they didn't give them the place they deserved. I wanted to express my opinion." Then, she added, "I'm sure you must know that my book was crowned by the French Academy." The last statement was added with much modesty. She told me that she needed to express her opinion particularly because she felt that the heroines were overlooked. Of one heroine named Pauline, she said, "That woman was very complex." Later, she added, "I was probably unconsciously drawn to women."

When I mentioned the contention of many male critics, in a 300 year tradition of patriarchal criticism, that the heroines were not as heroic as the heroes, she laughed and gave her opinion of male critics, "They often repeat themselves. I didn't agree with them; I preferred my interpretation. I found that justice was not rendered to the heroines, that they did not depict them as complex as they truly were." She also continued to make modest statements about her book such as, "I had little research to do because my book was, most of all, a personal interpretation; therefore, I had little research to do."

Maria Tastevin Miller was very resourceful and direct when it came time to submit her manuscript for publication. She chose Edouard Champion's publishing firm and went to see him personally. She knew he would be accessible. As she put it, "He received people easily. It wasn't difficult to speak to him." Champion agreed to publish her book and I am sure he thought his decision a shrewd one, when the French Academy crowned it less than one year after its publication.

I wondered about her biography and her teaching career, which I learned she pursued with much determination and courage. Although her parents did not oppose her teaching career, they made the following statement to warn her of the risk she was taking. "Vous vous déclassez," which can best be translated as, "You are lowering your social position," in other words, it will be harder for you to marry. Despite her parents' warning, the young Maria Tastevin pursued her love of learning and continued her studies until 1916, the year she passed the State examination for her "agrégation." The "agrégation" is a competitive examination conducted by the State for admission to posts on the teaching staff of "lycées" and universities.

World War I had a great impact on Maria Tastevin's teaching career. Shortly after completing her "agrégation," Tastevin was recruited by Smith College to teach French in the United States. Although she was excited by the offer, Maria Tastevin had to delay her plans, "It was during the war. I had a brother who was an aviator in the French Air Force, who might have been killed at any moment. I thought I could not leave my parents and go to the U.S.; therefore, I did not go to Smith." There was a little regret in her voice; however, she smiled and said, "But, that put the idea of Smith in my head." As a result, Tastevin accepted a teaching post from 1916 to 1918 at a girls' lycée in Niort, a small town in the southwest of France.

Once the war was over, however, Maria Tastevin's brother returned home, was soon married, and she said with a great deal of relief, "Now, I can go to the U.S." As she stated, "People spoke a lot about the U.S. I thought I would visit the U.S. for 18 months and return to France; however, once I was there, I decided to make a career for myself."

Maria Tastevin's first teaching post in the U.S. was at Stephens College in Columbia, Missouri. Again, she learned about the position through a recruiter. She accepted it in 1918 and left France without knowing anyone in the U.S. She spoke about her four years at Stephens with much fondness, "I had a lot of friends at Stephens, who adopted me as if I were their own daughter. I was very happy there." It was at Stephens that she joined the M.L.A. Eventually, it was through this organization that she learned of a Visiting Professorship at Vassar College. Although she hesitated at first to accept a temporary position, she believed, with her friends' assurances, that she would be able to find another job. As she stated, "I went to Vassar because it was Vassar. I really didn't want to leave my friends at Stephens College."

At Vassar, Maria Tastevin was an Assistant Professor of French from 1922 to 1923. Her first year went smoothly and her position became a permanent one. From 1923 to 1928, Tastevin was an Associate Professor who taught a full load of French language and literature courses, gave a lecture at Vassar entitled: "Women in France," and attended the M.L.A. conferences as a spectator, despite her active publication of scholarly articles in her field.

Although Maria Tastevin postponed marriage throughout the early years of her career, she met another professor of French, an American, during one of her numerous crossings of the Atlantic by ship, and decided to marry him in 1928. Tastevin was forty years old and her husband, John Richardson Miller, was in his forties, too.

After their marriage, Maria Tastevin resided in Paris on a two year leave of absence from Vassar. On September 1, 1928, she gave birth to a daughter named Madeleine-Marie. Her husband was in the U.S. at the time of his daughter's birth. Tastevin demonstrated her marvelous sense of humor, which remains intact today, when she sent him the following telegram through his employer, "Tell Miller, Madeleine wins." It was a comical way of informing him that instead of Paul, which was the name selected for a boy, the girl's name, Madeleine, won.

In 1930, the Miller family was reunited at Vassar. Maria Tastevin was accompanied by her daughter Madeleine, who was brought up on Vassar's campus. She also managed to have her husband hired to teach French at Vassar. From 1930 to 1931, she was hired as a Visiting Lecturer in French. The following year, she was promoted to Full Professor and retained that position until 1954, the year she she and her husband retired. Upon their retirement, they were both given Professor Emeritus status.

Although Tastevin stated that she never experienced discrmination, "because I was destined to a career of teaching women," she found that she had to be concerned about it with regard to her daughter's future. Madeleine Miller was a Class of 1951 Phi Beta Kappa graduate of Vassar. When Madeleine expressed an interest in medical school, her mother asked a local doctor in Poughkeepsie about schools to attend. He suggested Johns Hopkins University. When asked if there was discrimination against women there, he replied, "Not officially." Madeleine's plans for medical school were delayed. She returned to France and married a Frenchman in 1951.

The most painful event in Maria Tastevin's life occurred on December 25, 1952. Her daughter had married and given birth to a son in June of 1952. On Christmas morning, after midnight mass, Madeleine and her husband were on their way to a festive family dinner. They had left their son, Paul, at home with a baby sitter. Madeleine and her husband had a car accident and she was killed instantly. Her husband, who was driving, survived. Maria Tastevin's voice still quivers when she speaks of that tragic night in her life. "I suffered a lot when my daughter was killed. It was as if a bombshell had dropped on my life. We couldn't predict it. Madeleine was 23 years old and her son was six months when she died. She left me a son, at least." Despite the irreparable loss that both she and her husband suffered, they remained at Vassar for two years after their daughter's death.

Today, Maria Tastevin sits in her apartment in Paris surrounded by many family portraits, the most striking one being of her daughter, Madeleine. It's a large 8 by 10 Polaroid portrait taken in 1949, "it was one of the first Polaroid pictures produced," she says with pride.

In the thirty years since her departure from Vassar College and the U.S., she has led an active intellectual life. Her two favorite areas for reading are in the fields of history and literary criticism. In 1983, when I asked her what she was reading, she said, "a brilliant biography of Sophie Trébuchet, Victor Hugo's mother, by Geneviève Dormann," which substantiates her continued interest in strong,

197

willful, and determined women.

At the conclusion of the interview, I told her that her book had helped me a lot, and she said, "I'm happy if that's true." I also told her that I was going to write an article about her, and she said, "Not about me. I hope you are going to choose other women, too. Not just me."

Despite the fact that Maria Tastevin has been categorically, if not, deliberately ignored by male scholars who have invested their energies in the quest of the Cornelian hero, her contribution to feminist criticism and the role of the heroine in the Cornelian canon, can no longer be overlooked. Her insights and literary criticism were of a feminist nature before feminist criticism existed. She should be applauded for the courage of her convictions, particularly because she lived without the benefit of a community of feminist critics, and because she was able to operate against the tide of an oppressive negation of the role of women characters in literature.

*All translations of Maria Tastevin Miller's quotes were done by Josephine A. Schmidt.

ABOUT THE AUTHOR

Josephine A. Schmidt is an Assistant Professor of French at California State College, Bakersfield. She also teaches Spanish and Women's Studies at CSB. She received the B.A. from Chestnut Hill College, the M.A. from the University of Virginia, and the Ph.D. from the University of Virginia. Before assuming her present post she was an Assistant Professor of French and Spanish at Cedar Crest College.